"Mother Loyola has won enviable distinction as a writer of books which treat of the spiritual life. Her mind is vigorous, her heart is large, her information is accurate, her style is refined and vivid, and her pen is easy—all these qualities combine to give her works a high rank in Catholic devotional literature. Few writers in English have fathomed as she has fathomed the depth of the treasures contained in the Holy Eucharist and the solemn preparation that should be made for a worthy reception of our Lord in Holy Communion....To help us speak this "welcome" reverently and heartfully, tenderly and fervently, is the object of this exquisite book which is full of vigorous thought and of sturdy emotion. It will always be a most acceptable gift to devout souls, but, above all, to those who are serving God in the sanctuary of religion."

—from a review of *Welcome!* in Donahoe's Magazine,
November 1904.

My delights were to be with the children of men.
(Prov. 8:31.)

Welcome!

Holy Communion:

Before and After

by

Mother Mary Loyola

edited by

Rev. Herbert Thurston, S.J.

2015
ST. AUGUSTINE ACADEMY PRESS
HOMER GLEN, ILLINOIS

Nihil Obstat:

    HERBERT THURSTON, S.J.

3rd April 1904.

Imprimatur:

    ✠FRANCISCUS,

                Archiep. Westmonast.

Die 4 Aprilis 1904.

ISBN: 978-1-936639-35-9

Library of Congress Control Number: 2015943308

*And the Spirit and the Bride say
Come!*

*And he that heareth let him say
Come!*

Amen. Come, Lord Jesus!

CONTENTS

PREFACE

HOWEVER sincere may be the often-expressed distaste for artificial forms of prayer, there is, if I mistake not, deep down in human nature a certain instinctive craving for the adequate expression of its needs and emotions. We do not want to memorialise the Almighty in the language appropriate to a civic address, but, on the other hand, we are not always quite content to use the simple formulae or the stumbling improvisations of spiritual childhood. We feel that something more is expected of us—otherwise, why lift our voices in supplication at all to the God who already knows what we crave? Our moods are very various, our thoughts about God and our own souls are often more entangled than our ideas about anything else in the world. The spiritual guide who helps us most is he who can interpret ourselves to ourselves; and to nobody do we feel a deeper gratitude than to one who can put into simple words the vague longings after good which we know not how to utter in any form that satisfies us. Thus, our objection to written prayers arises not so much from the fact that reading our petitions makes them unreal, as because we so rarely meet with a book that says just what we want to say, and says it worthily in terms that ring natural and true.

After all, the Church has always encouraged the use of forms of prayer—at least to aid and supplement private devotion. During penitential seasons we still retain in our liturgy the traces of an interesting practice of the early ages, which Mgr. Duchesne has aptly designated *l'oraison collective*. In this the President of any Christian assembly, after a subject had been announced to the congregation present and a space of time had been left them for private recollection upon their knees, rose to his feet and summed up in a few aptly chosen words the vaguely formed hopes and desires arising in the hearts of each. It seems to me that Mother Loyola in this little volume of Preparations and Thanksgivings for Holy Communion has discharged much the same function for her pious readers. There will be many, if I mistake not, who will find here the expression of what they have often deeply felt and been unable to put satisfactorily into words for themselves. But there will also be others for whom its most useful function will be to suggest and to stimulate, and this latter service, as the more important of the two, is also, I understand, the more directly designed by the author. It has not been her idea to furnish, as in a prayer-book, all the acts usual before and after Holy Communion, but rather to propose a dominant thought, to fall in with a mood, or need, or burden. "For the rest," she writes, "the soul should be left to shape its own prayer, in words more fruitful, because more direct and intimate, than any that could be provided from without." There is no reason to doubt that those who use this little book in this spirit will find it both immediately and permanently helpful as an aid to their devotion in Holy Communion.

HERBERT THURSTON, S.J.
31 Farm Street W.,
Feast of the Patronage of St. Joseph,
1904

INTRODUCTION

MANY circumstances will determine the character of our preparation for the visit of a guest—his rank, his relations with us, the object of his visit, and perhaps our special needs at the time. But one disposition will ensure its fitness and acceptableness in every case. Let him but hear "Welcome" from our lips, or rather see "Welcome" in our face, and he will be satisfied. "Welcome!" greets the sovereign in letters of light. It is seemly on the lips of the poorest peasant, of the casual acquaintance, of the intimate friend, of the parent, and of the child. It never tires, it never grows monotonous or superfluous. For it takes a new meaning with every change of circumstance affecting our guest or ourselves. If either is joyous or sad, wronged, weary, anxious, burdened, disturbed—it suits itself to every need. Our Lord is one of us and like us in all things, sin excepted. His

Heart responds like ours to the sound of "Welcome!"
It beat quicker as, tired at evening with His daily toil,
He crossed the threshold of His home at Nazareth
and read it in Mary's face. As He saw it stamped
clear and bright all the house over at Bethany. As He
heard Martha's greeting, reverent yet hearty, and her
sister's whisper inaudible to all but Him.

So sweet to His ear is its sound that He condescends
to invite it: "Zacheus, make haste and come down, for
this day I must abide in thy house. And he came down
and received Him with joy." "And they drew nigh to
the town whither they were going, and He made as
though He would go farther. But they constrained
Him, saying: Stay with us, because it is towards
evening, and the day is now far spent. And He went
in with them."

On the other hand, how He feels the absence of
welcome, how sensitive He is to mere outward forms
of decorum: "Thou gavest Me no kiss!" We know,
then, what to secure when He comes to us, what will
make His visit a pleasure to Him. For this, surely, is
our chief aim in our Communions. We go to Him to
be fed, enriched, comforted, no doubt. But there is a
stronger reason still, a deeper need to be satisfied. We
have to make Him a return of love. We have to receive
with joy the Guest whose delight is to be with us.

Our welcome, as we have seen, will vary in character with our dominant disposition at the time. It will be jubilant or humble, wistful, sympathetic, or grateful, as praise, contrition, desire, trust, love, sway us at the time. But all will be variations of one chord. And each a fresh title to His own "Welcome!" on the threshold of our Home. Coming out of the darkness of this world, we shall see Him standing there awaiting us. He has been our welcome Guest times without number during the days of our pilgrimage; the hour has come for us to be His. "Come, blessed of My Father, possess you the Kingdom prepared for you from the foundation of the world. . . . Enter thou into the joy of thy Lord."

THE WELCOME OF MARY

THE WELCOME OF MARY

"I will joy in God my Jesus"—Habacuc 3:18.

WHAT a model we have in Mary's welcome! What beautiful commingling of adoration and affection! The folding of her Divine Child to her breast on Christmas night was the fond embrace of the Mother, but it was no less the worship and the clinging of the creature.

What annihilation of self in His Presence, what concentration on Him of all her powers, what whole-hearted jubilant praise, what joyous offers of service, what glowing gratitude welcomed Him in the Incarnation, at the Nativity, in every Communion at the hands of John during the years in Ephesus and Jerusalem!

The reception of a king, a father, a conqueror, a benefactor, a friend, a bridegroom, a child, has each its special characteristic. Christ was all these to Mary and more a thousand times. She had to give Him, as far as in her lay, the welcome due to a God. Was she equal to this? Her mind and heart were at home in regions to which the most daring flight of the cherubim and seraphim never attained. But when she crossed her hands upon her breast after Communion, and bowed down in adoration, she felt as no other creature has ever felt, and acknowledged in depths of humility, of which we do not so much as dream, the utter insufficiency of her worship and her love.

Mary knew that He who is mighty had done great things for her. And she knew that the return to Him of all He had given fell short of what was due to Him by a deficit that was simply infinite. Around her on every side stretched a limitless ocean of perfection which no human praise could cover. She tried unceasingly to meet its claims upon her homage, and incessantly fell back upon her nothingness as a creature. Yet not to rest there. For in the Treasure confided to her in the Incarnation and in the Eucharist, she had enough, more than enough, to supply all her deficiency. She had the Co-equal Son to offer to the Father as her adoration, and thanksgiving, and praise.

The same treasure is made over to us. Like Mary, we make such return from our own store as we may. And then, conscious that we are unprofitable servants, "wretched and miserable, and poor and blind," we have recourse, like her, to the Infinite God within our breast, and offer Him to Himself as a Welcome worthy of Him.

Mary most holy, I come to thee in my great need. I am preparing to receive into my heart the Holy of Holies, and, dear Mother, I am afraid. I know His eyes cannot endure iniquity. I know that in His Angels He found sin. I know that He sees and sounds to its depths my sinful soul. And still He bids me come to Him and be united to Him in the closest union possible upon earth. How shall I stand before the Most High? How shall I, a sinner, dare to draw near to Him before whom the spotless Angels veil their faces and sing continually "Holy, Holy, Holy"?

Blessed be His love and His compassion. He Himself has prepared my way to Him. He has made the conditions so easy, that I can have no excuse for keeping at a distance and declining His invitation to "sup with Him." The wedding garment of grace— this is all He strictly requires. Less He could not ask. Anything more He leaves to my love and sense of fitness. Thy immaculate purity, thy glorious holiness were not too much by way of preparation for Him—and He is content with such poor dispositions as I can bring.

He will Himself give me the wedding garment; and to make up for the ornaments of grace so sadly wanting, He bids me betake myself to those who can help me from their abundance. Patriarchs, Prophets, Apostles, Martyrs, Confessors, Virgins, Angels, Archangels, Cherubim, Seraphim—the whole heavenly host, by the Communion of Saints, is at my service. And, most willing of all to help, the kindest, the most approachable, is the highest of all His holy ones. Though Mother of God and Queen of Heaven, she remembers that she is my Mother, and thinks it the simplest thing in the world to stoop from her throne in order to succour me in my need. As a mother decks her child in her own jewels that she may appear fittingly at court, so does my Mother make over to me all I ask for or desire, that I may be pleasing in the sight of the King of kings.

Give me, then, dear Mother, all thou seest me to need. I am so poor and ignorant that I do not even know what is lacking to me. Give me of thy treasures. Thou wilt not, like the prudent virgins, send me elsewhere to beg. For thou hast enough for thyself and for me. Thou art the dispenser of the good things of God, the neck through which all virtue flows to the members from their Head. Get me, then, a share in the graces that enriched thy soul and made it so beautiful in the eyes of God; in the faith that no trial could stagger; in the hope that clung closer to God for every blow; in the love that was absolutely self-forgetting and ready for every sacrifice. Above all, get me the humility that more than any other grace found thee favour with the Most High, that ought to come naturally to me, that more than all others I have need to ask.

And, Mother, get me thy desires. My heart is cold, unstirred, even by the beauty and attractiveness of thy Divine Son, even by His own desire to be with me. Show me—show me here and now the blessed Fruit of thy womb, Jesus, that I may be drawn to love Him and to make Him welcome at His coming.

Come, Lord Jesus, come! Come and find me prepared by Thy Mother's hands for union with Thee. Consider in me, not my own poverty, but the riches that from her heart have passed to mine.

After Communion

"My soul doth magnify the Lord, and my spirit hath rejoiced in God my Saviour" (Luke 1:46-47).

"For He that is mighty hath done great things to me, and holy is His Name" (Luke 1:49).

"Bless the Lord, all ye His angels, you that are mighty in strength" (Ps 102: 20).

"O magnify the Lord with me, and let us extol His name together" (Ps 33:4).

"For this is God, our God unto eternity, and for ever and ever" (Ps 47:15).

"Give praise to our God, all ye His servants, and you that fear Him, little and great" (Apoc. 19:5).

"Sing praises to our God, sing ye; sing praises to our King, sing ye" (Ps. 46:7).

"For this is God, our God unto eternity, and for ever and ever" (Ps 47:15).

"Blessed be the Lord God this day" (3 Kings 5:7).

"Amen. Benediction, and glory, and thanksgiving, honour, and power, and strength to our God for ever and ever. Amen" (Apoc. 7:12).

"For this is God, our God unto eternity, and for ever and ever" (Ps 47:15).

I wish, my God, I could give Thee the best of welcomes. I unite my poor feeble welcome to the welcome of Mary in the Incarnation—to her welcome on Christmas night when she first folded Thee to her breast—to her welcome when she found Thee after a three days' loss—to her welcome each evening as she received Thee home from Thy daily toil—to her welcome as she held out her arms to receive Thee from the cross—to her ecstasy of welcome when Thou camest to her at sunrise on Easter Day—to her daily welcome when she received Thee, like us, beneath the veils during the years that followed the Ascension, when her life was sustained by Thy sacramental Presence—to her welcome that was the reflex of Thine own when she was received into Thine embrace on the day of her Assumption.

Oh that, even at an immeasurable distance, I could follow her lead in the adoration, the praise, the sympathy, the reparation, the conformity of will and mind and heart which united her to Thee and were the solace and the joy of Thy Sacred Human Heart!

I, too, would shelter Thee, Lord, from the coldness of the winter night, not only by receiving Thee into my heart, but by taking to my heart Thy suffering members, by feeding, clothing, harbouring them of whom Thou hast said: "Whatsoever you do to one of My least brethren you do it unto Me" (Matt. 25:40).

I, too, will seek Thee when Thou hidest from me, either in just punishment for past sin, or for present carelessness in Thy service. I will seek Thee wherever through negligence I may have lost

Thee. I will review my use of the Sacraments, my hearing of Holy Mass; the duties of my state; my responsibility towards those entrusted to me, of whom I shall have to render an account to Thee; the result of my example on my household. I will humble myself before Thee when I find that through my fault I have deserved to forfeit the sense of Thy Presence. If I cannot trace to any special cause Thy absence from me, I will humble myself for my hidden faults. For though "I am not conscious to myself of anything, yet am I not hereby justified, for He that judgeth me is the Lord" (1 Cor. 4:4). In Thy Blessed Mother there was nothing calling for chastisement or for purification. Only for the increase of her merit was the pain of the three days' loss. In my case the subtraction of Thy sensible Presence has a threefold cause and fruit. See, Lord, that I profit by it according to Thy designs. I accept it in punishment of my sins, for the purification of my imperfect love, and for the increase of my merit. Let weary search for Thee here bring greater nearness to Thee hereafter. Let me seek, like Thy Blessed Mother, till I find. Let me find Thee whom my soul loveth when the day breaks and the shadows retire, and for all eternity I will not let Thee go.

Oblation and Petition

Thou hast revealed Thyself to me, my God, as Love. And because it is the nature of love to give, Thou givest prodigally, untiringly, of Thy best. "God so loved the world as to give His only-begotten Son" (John 3:16). All other gifts are less than this. All others are contained in this. "How hath He not also with Him given us all things?" (Rom. 8:32).

What can I give Thee in return? I have nothing but what is Thine. But Thou wilt accept from my hand what is already Thy own. I offer to Thee, then, and return to Thee all Thy gifts of body or of soul, all that Love has given, all it has withheld—life, strength, aptitudes, limitations; my trials, my joys, my graces, my responsibilities, my desires, my capabilities of serving Thee. And since all I have is unworthy of Thy acceptance, I offer Thee the virtues and merits of all the Angels and Saints. I offer Thee the heart of Mary most holy. I offer Thee Thy own most sacred Heart, an offering of infinite worth, made over to me in Holy Communion that I may present it to Thee again, a more than sufficient return for all I have received, for all I expect here and hereafter.

I offer Thee this Sacred Heart for every soul in the world today; for the five hundred millions of Christians, of whom so many bear Thy Name without loving or serving Thee; for the nine hundred millions who have never heard Thy Name, to whom the beauty of Thy life and the tenderness of Thy Heart have never been made known. O Redeemer of men, who willest not the death of any, but that all should be converted and live, save these perishing souls, each one of whom is purchased with Thy Precious Blood, each one of whom has its place in Thy Heart. O Lord of the harvest, send forth labourers into Thy harvest. Let the Faith spread more widely and more quickly. Prosper the foreign missions; secure baptism for dying infants; succour those who will die today, unhelped by priest or sacraments.

I offer Thy Sacred Heart for all who are groping their way to the truth. O Light that enlightenest every man that cometh into this world, help them through difficulties which Thou alone canst measure and remove. Strengthen those who are hesitating on the threshold of the Church, those whom temporal motives hold back. Oh that I might be so happy as to assist even one of these souls! Lord, give me the opportunity and the grace. Let me do a little if I cannot do much. Make me generous with sympathy, time, whatever I can place at their service. And count every effort, every desire, as an act of thanksgiving for the gift of faith bestowed so undeservedly on me.

Prayer before a Crucifix

A plenary indulgence, applicable to the souls in Purgatory, was granted by Pope Pius VII, to all the faithful who, after having confessed their sins with contrition, received Holy Communion, and prayed for the intentions of the Sovereign Pontiff, shall devoutly recite the following prayer before an image or representation of Christ crucified.

BEHOLD, O kind and most sweet Jesus, I cast myself upon my knees in Thy sight, and with the most fervent desire of my soul I pray and beseech Thee that Thou wouldst impress upon my heart lively sentiments of faith, hope, and charity, with true repentance for my sins, and a firm desire of amendment, whilst, with deep affection and grief of soul, I ponder within myself and mentally contemplate Thy five most precious wounds, having before my eyes that which David spake in prophecy: *"They pierced my hands and my feet, they have numbered all my bones."*

Say five times the Our Father *and* Hail Mary *for the Pope and the wants of the Church.*

THE WELCOME OF FAITH

THE WELCOME OF FAITH

I

"Blessed are they that have not seen and have believed"
—John 20:29.

Before Communion

NOTHING can suppress the longing desire of some of us to have lived in the time of our Lord. We may be shown our greater advantages, but the feeling remains that had we been able to kneel at His feet, to meet the glance of His eye, to hear His voice, we should have been drawn to Him irresistibly and have loved Him with a devotedness which, alas! we are sadly conscious is wanting now.

Two thoughts may turn to account this harmless if not very profitable desire.

Let us transport ourselves in spirit to some spot where the Christian faith has not as yet been planted, but where some knowledge of Christ has reached, and imagine our lot to have been cast there. We have heard some fragments of the Gospel story, and how Christ, having finished the work of man's redemption, still dwelt on earth in Christian lands to be the consolation and help of His followers to the end of time. That there the Sacrifice of Calvary was daily renewed for the washing away of daily sin. That there, though His face was not seen nor His voice heard, His Real Presence in the churches perpetuated His life and healing work among men. That He was there day and night to welcome all comers; to listen with the same pitifulness as of old; to comfort, to bless, and help all who approached Him. What would be the longing of our hearts to have been born in one of those favoured lands where we might have been numbered among His disciples, as truly as in the time of our Lord!

Again. Let us transport ourselves in thought to a place which by God's mercy we all hope to reach some day—the land of fierce suffering and weary waiting—the land of Purgatory. What, as we lie there in our helplessness, shall we think of the Tabernacle and the altar rails, of that "day of the Lord" when we were free to come and go in His Presence, to pour out our

hearts before Him, to seek His help in every need!
No heart has ever longed for the visible Presence of
Jesus during the Three and Thirty Years as we shall
long for the old graces in Mass and Communion in
the time forever passed away.

Shall we not profit by it while it lasts? "Behold
now is the acceptable time: behold now is the day of
salvation" (2 Cor. 6:2). "Didst thou but know the
Gift of God," our Lord says to us, "there would be no
room for hankering for the days of old, for Judea or
Galilee." Here on the altar is Bethlehem and Calvary.
Here at the communion rails we may welcome Jesus of
Nazareth when we will, and fold Him to our heart,
and cast ourselves upon His.

Oh that I realised my own privileges as fully as I
appreciate those of others! Why should I envy the
Jewish crowds, or the little household at Bethany,
or even the Twelve? I have Thy words, dear Lord,
to instruct and warm my heart, and, happier than
the people of Thy own land, I can ponder them at
leisure in the sacred pages that have preserved them
for me. The very sound of Thy voice I may catch
now and again in "*Talitha, cumi;*" "*Eloi, Eloi, lamma
sabacthani!*" I may come to Thee amid the bustle

and heat of the day, or in the silence of night, to lay before Thee the perplexities, the eager questionings, the many needs of my soul. I may follow Thee from place to place like the holy women, showing my love in practical form by ministering of my substance to Thee and Thine. I may receive Thee under my roof like the sisters at Bethany, and hear Thy words of love, or gentle warning, or reproach. I may commend to Thee in their need those who are dear to me and to Thee, and with loving familiarity expostulate with Thee when Thou dost delay to hear my prayer. I may weep with Thee over the graves that have taken from me my dearest and my best, and listen with Martha to the promise that they shall be mine again one day. In my hours of desolation I may kneel beside Thee in the Garden and unite my petition with Thy strong cry and tears. When passion agitates me I may hasten to the pillar of the scourging or to the cross of shame, and draw into my soul the meekness of Thine. In every need Thy followers and Thy friends had recourse to Thee whilst Thou wert on earth. I may do the same. One thing alone is needed—faith. *Sola fides sufficit.* Faith alone suffices. Lord, increase my faith!

AFTER COMMUNION

Tantum ergo Sacramentum
Veneremur cernui:
> Down in adoration falling,
> Lo! the Sacred Host we hail;

Praestet fides supplementum
Sensuum defectui.
> Faith for all defects supplying
> Where the feeble senses fail.

Adoro te devote, latens Deitas,
Quae sub his figuris vere latitas.
> In loving adoration unto Thee,
> O Hidden God, I humbly bend my knee;
> Beneath these lowly semblances concealed,
> To senses hid, to Faith alone revealed.

Plagas, sicut Thomas, non intucor,
Deum tamen meum te confiteor;
Fac me tibi semper magis credere,
In te spem habere, te diligere.
> I cannot see Thee, Jesu glorified,
> Nor touch Thy wounded hands and riven side;
> Yet with St. Thomas at Thy feet I fall,
> And worship Thee, "My Lord, my God, my all."[1]

"Blessed are they that have not seen and have believed." Yet Thou hadst said, dear Lord, "Blessed are the eyes that see the things that you see." Truly blessed were the eyes that saw what kings and prophets had longed

---

1 Fr. Tyrrell, S.J.

to see, the Face that Angels desire to see. What, then, must be the happiness which transcends blessedness such as this—what my happiness now! What the reward of faith when, the time of trial over, the veils drop and it meets Thee face to face!

And faith is blessed even now. For its patience, its hope, its strong anchorage on God in spite of difficulties and obscurities and the human pride which resents these things—all this is worship. It is the worship of Himself that God has chosen. From the beginning, O Lord, Thou hast made faith the road of access to Thee, and the only road. Along that path all Thy holy ones have journeyed. It was in reward of their faith that the blind saw, the deaf heard, the lepers were cleansed during Thy life on earth; that sinners through all time have been forgiven; that the just have persevered to the end. If I believe, and in proportion to my belief, I may hope great things of Thee. Lord, increase my faith. Give me the faith of the generations of saints who never looked upon Thy face on earth—the faith of Agnes, and Augustine, and Teresa, and Thomas of Aquin, and Ignatius. They are my brothers and sisters in the Kingdom of God, not separated from me by an impassable chasm, but linked with me like travellers on the same road, ready to bear me up when I stumble or falter, to sustain me when I faint, to speak to me in hours of darkness of the light on the other side of the distant hills. Like me they once walked by faith. They had their seasons of trial and depression. They were supported all through their pilgrimage on earth by the Sacramental Presence that is with me now.

Lord, increase my faith. With Thomas I fall down before Thee, my Lord and my God. With Peter and with Martha I acknowledge Thee for the Christ, the Son of the living God. Let nothing ever cloud my faith. Rather let it go on brightening till it brings me into the perfect Day. May every genuflection before Thy Tabernacle, every visit to Thee, every reception of Thee, glorify Thee by my faith. I am glad, my God, to give Thee the submission of my mind no less than the love of my heart. I am glad to serve Thee at my own cost for the little space of my life on earth. Only up to the gates of eternity wilt Thou ask for my faith. Once within those gates—what a change, what a revelation! My eyes shall see the King in His Beauty. I shall see Thy glory, and be satisfied. As I fall before Thine unveiled Face, how I shall thank Thee for the gift of faith on earth!

Jesu, quem velatum nunc aspicio,
Oro, fiat illud quod tam sitio;
Ut te revelata cernens facie,
Visu sim beatus tuae gloriae.

O Jesu, whom by faith I now descry,
Veiled as Thou liest here from mortal eye;
When wilt Thou grant the longing of my heart,
Thirsting to see and know Thee as Thou art:
To see Thee face to face in endless day,
When Faith shall cease and shadows flee away;
To share Thy Blessedness without alloy,
To glory in Thy glory and Thy joy![1]

Oblation and Petition, p. 10.

Prayer before a Crucifix, p. 12.

---

1   Fr. Tyrrell, S.J.

THE WELCOME OF FAITH

II

"Lord, I believe; help Thou mine unbelief."

Before Communion

FAITH, a lively faith, would cure all our spiritual diseases and supply all our needs. It was the one thing our Lord required in those who came to Him petitioning for favours when He was on earth. It is what He wants of us all now. "He could not do many miracles there because of their unbelief," we are told, as if this evil disposition tied His hands and restricted even His Omnipotence. On the other hand, He said to the father who implored Him to heal his lunatic son: "If thou canst believe, all things are possible to them that believe." He speaks as if the answer to our prayers was in our own hands rather than in His. This poor father had said: "If Thou canst do anything, help us, having compassion on us. Jesus said to him: If thou canst believe, all things are possible. Immediately the father of the boy, crying out with tears, said: I do believe; Lord, help my unbelief. And the child was cured from that hour."

From our Lord's words we see that He knows faith is a difficulty to us; that He tries to bring us to a lively faith by holding out its reward; that faith obtains all it wills from Him.

He understands the difficulty faith is to us. Hemmed in as we are by the things of sense, it is hard to realise that these are not what we take them to be; that though we see and handle them every day, and they seem solid and lasting, they are as shadows compared with things unseen, the realities amid which we shall be living before many years are passed.

It is hard to bring home to ourselves the fact that day and night, sleeping and waking, we are under the Eye of One who is more present to us than we are to ourselves. That in Him we live and move, and are, and employ every faculty of soul and body. That leaving to us the unfettered exercise of freewill, His Providence overrules all our actions to the accomplishment of its designs. That it permits pain, sorrow, moral evil even, and makes all work together for the good of the elect. That not a hair of our head falls to the ground without

His knowledge. That little and miserable as we know ourselves to be, we are unspeakably dear and precious in the sight of our Heavenly Father, always welcome when we come to Him, and never more so than when we bring Him sin to be forgiven.

It is hard to realise that the same blessed Presence that sanctified the cottage of Nazareth is in every Catholic church today; not in figure, but in deed and in truth. That He who walked by the Lake with His twelve chosen companions, ate and drank with them, slept when He was weary, prayed when He was in trouble, wept when He had lost a friend, came joyfully where a welcome awaited Him, sorrowed when His own received Him not—that He is still on earth, in our midst, Body and Blood and Soul and Divinity, unchanged in character, with the same tenderness and affection that endeared Him to the friends of His life on earth.

These truths are hard to grasp with the living hold that makes them part of ourselves. Hence our Lord says to us: "If thou canst believe." What have we in answer but the words of the Jewish father: "I do believe; Lord, help mine unbelief."

He is ready and glad to help, but here, as everywhere, His way is to help those who help themselves. How do we help ourselves? By the quiet pondering of what we hold by faith. It is not the effort to excite devotional feeling that He asks of us, but the pondered act of faith. Close to my heart after Communion is the Heart that loved me unto death; that has spent itself for me in all manner of labours and sacrifices; that has employed every winning device to gain my love; that has been pained by my ingratitude; that asks me now to make amends for the past by returning it love for love. Can I make my act of faith as to these motives one by one, and not desire at least to make Him the return He asks?

My God, I most firmly believe that I am about to hold within my heart that Heart of Thine which loved me unto the death of the cross. I believe in its love for me. Not all my weakness and unworthiness, not all my falls shall make me doubt Thy love. It is for such as I am that the miracle of the Blessed Sacrament is wrought. It is to bring within my reach a remedy for every need of my soul. I believe, Lord, I believe; help Thou my unbelief. Thou knowest my difficulties better than I know them myself. Thou knowest how the cares of this life, which I take up every morning, weigh me down and absorb my thoughts, and leave but little room for the memory of Thee and the things that concern my soul. It is for this very reason that I come to Thee. It is to cast all my care on Thee; to put my soul into Thy keeping; to trust to Thee my trials and temptations, the busy hand and brain, all my life's work to be lifted up and made holy and meritorious for heaven by union with Thine, by being done for Thee. I believe in Thy Real Presence because Thou hast said it. Remember Thy word: "All things are possible to him that believeth," and let the healing of my soul be the reward of my faith.

AFTER COMMUNION

I bow myself down to adore Thee, O God my Saviour, the same who at the word: "Lord, I believe," didst heal the Jewish father's afflicted child—the very same. Lord, I believe, and falling down I adore Thee.

"Adore Him, all you His angels" (Ps 96:7).

"Exalt ye the Lord our God" (Ps. 98:9).

"Adore the Lord our God and give thanks to Him" (Tobias 11:7).

"Give praise to our God, all ye His servants, and you that fear Him, little and great" (Apoc. 19:5).

"Sing praises to our God, sing ye; sing praises to our King, sing ye" (Ps. 46:7).

"For this is God, our God unto eternity, and for ever and ever" (Ps. 47:15).

"Thou art worthy, O Lord our God, to receive glory, and honour, and power" (Apoc. 4:11).

"Amen. Benediction, and glory, and thanksgiving, honour, and power, and strength to our God for ever and ever. Amen" (Apoc. 7:12).

Thy healing touch, O Lord, which did so much for that poor suffering boy, can do much for me. I believe it will do much. I hope in Thee, building my trust on Thy compassion and Thy love. Suffering and troubled, I place myself beneath Thy hands. "If Thou canst do anything," said the boy's father. I know, O Lord, that Thou canst do all things, that it will cost Thee but a word to help me. I know too that Thou art more eager to give Thy help than I am to ask it. I love and thank Thee for Thy goodness, and commit myself to Thee.

Thanks be to Thee for the unmerited gift of faith to which I owe Thy Real Presence with me now. Lord, increase my faith, for in proportion as it grows, will hope and love grow with it. Help me to lead a life worthy of my faith, a life permeated and vivified throughout by faith. Give me faith to see Thy hand in all that happens, to turn suffering to profit, to look at the passing things of time in the light of eternity, and live for the life that is to come.

"Lord, increase our faith." This was the prayer of Thy Apostles, the prayer of all the Saints. All their grand service of Thee, all their merits, all the power of their prayer, their influence for good, their love of Thee here, their joy in Thee throughout eternity, sprang from that germ, small once as the grain of mustard seed, the faith of their baptism, the faith of the one true Church.

I too am a child of the Church. I too have the faith once delivered to the Saints. My God, let it fructify in my heart as in theirs. Increase my faith. Give me the faith that will remove mountains, that will clear away every obstacle between myself and Thee, that will win from Thee at last that word of praise—"Great is thy faith."

Oblation and Petition, p. 10.

Prayer before a Crucifix, p. 12.

THE WELCOME OF A
CREATURE

THE WELCOME OF A CREATURE

I

*"Know, therefore, this day, and think in thy heart,
that the Lord He is God."*—Deut. 4:39.

Before Communion

HEREIN is my fittest, most fruitful preparation for Communion, commended to me by God Himself—to ponder in my heart this tremendous truth, that He who comes to me—is God!

Thou art small, my heart, very small; there is no room in thee at this moment for any other thought, if this thought so high, so deep, so vast on every side, is to enter in and take possession of thee. Cast out, then, all images of this earth; curtain closely the entrance to His sanctuary, that no noise from without may reach to trouble thee. Concentrate all thy powers upon this thought—He who comes to thee is God: who had no beginning; to whom all time is a point; who inhabits light inaccessible; who, in a sense, has no perfections, but is Himself the one infinite Perfection.

"Maker of heaven and earth and of all things visible and invisible." "The Lord of the whole creation" (Judith 9:17); in whom are found as in their principle the types of all created, of all possible things. "Behold, heaven is the Lord thy God's, and the heaven of heavens, the earth, and all things that are therein" (Deut. 10:14). Of whom are all form and colour; all harmony and fragrance; all goodness, and truth, and beauty; all majesty and holiness; all love and fidelity; all tenderness and sweetness; all restfulness and peace—whatsoever of fairness and fecundity and beneficence is possessed by created things; "who is over all things, God blessed forever" (Rom. 9:5).

He who comes to me is Jesus Christ, "the Only-Begotten Son of God, born of the Father before all ages; God of God; Light of Light; very God of very God; begotten, not made; consubstantial with the Father; by whom all things were made. Who for us men, and for our salvation, descended from heaven. And was incarnate by the Holy Ghost of the Virgin Mary; and was made man. Was crucified also for us; suffered under Pontius Pilate and was buried. And the third day He rose again, according to the Scriptures. And ascended into heaven; sits at the right hand of the Father. And again He shall come with glory to judge the living and the dead; of whose kingdom there shall be no end."

He comes, who to save me, and win me, and bring me to His kingdom took my nature, and in that nature suffered, and in that nature waits for me now at the right hand of the Father. For me, as if there were no other, He was made man. For me, as if there were no other, he laid down His life upon the cross. F or me He rose again and ascended into heaven. For me He pleads there and prepares my place. "Behold thy Saviour cometh" (Isa. 62:11). "Amen. Come, Lord Jesus" (Apoc. 22:20).

He who comes to me is "the Lord and life-giver; who proceeds from the Father and the Son; who together with the Father and the Son is adored and glorified." "My Spirit shall be in the midst of you; fear not" (Aggeus 2:6). "The Spirit of the Lord shall come upon thee, and thou shalt be changed into another man" (1 Kings 10:6).

"Oh how hast Thou multiplied Thy mercy, O God" (Ps. 35:8).

"What shall I render to the Lord for all that He hath rendered to me?" (Ps. 115:12).

"Let all Thy works, O Lord, praise Thee, and let all Thy saints bless Thee" (Ps. 144:10).

AFTER COMMUNION

Glory to God in the highest

Glory to God for a condescension greater than the humiliations of Bethlehem or of Calvary. For beneath the swathing bands, and on the cross, there was a self-assertion and a freedom He has denied Himself in the Host. There He had the worship of Mary, the love and loyalty of a few faithful souls. But here! Lord, whence is this to me that Thou shouldst come to me? Glory to Thee in the highest, in the Bosom of the Father from eternity. Glory to Thee in the lowest abasement to which Thy love constrains Thee, in Thy coming today—to me.

And on earth peace to men of goodwill.

Peace to this soul of mine to which the Prince of Peace has come.

Peace; for with all my poverty, weakness and inconstancy, I hope I have goodwill. On this Thou canst build, O Lord; if I can bring Thee this, Thou wilt be content. But goodwill, to be genuine, must follow the lead of Thy grace, must be ready for effort and self-sacrifice. And I am weak. Give me strength, O Lord. I have desires as Thou knowest, but when the time comes for action, when opportunities offer of serving Thee at my own cost, I hang back. And so I am forever "halting between two sides" (3 Kings 18:21), uneasy, dissatisfied, for who hath resisted Thee and hath had peace? I ask for strength, O Lord. Thou hast given me desires; give me what is as easy to Thee to give—the force to carry them into effect. So shall I deserve the peace promised to men of goodwill.

> *We praise Thee; we bless Thee;*
> *we adore Thee; we glorify Thee.*

"I and my soul will rejoice in Him," said Tobias (Tobias 13:9). As if in the fullness of his heart he would multiply himself that he might multiply praise; desiring impossibilities, like Mary when she would magnify the Lord. I and my soul will rejoice in Thee, O God my Saviour, here truly present with me. We praise Thee for what Thou art in Thyself. We bless Thee for all Thou art to us. We adore Thee as our Creator and our God, as the "most mighty God" (Gen. 46:3); "Lord of the whole creation" (Judith 9:17); "Who hast made heaven and earth and all things that are under the cope of heaven" (Esther 13:10). We glorify Thee as an Infant laid in a manger. And in that last resort of Thy condescension, the Host within my breast.

We give Thee thanks for Thy great glory.

For Thine infinite compassion for the work of Thy hands, and the marvels Thou hast wrought for us in Thy Redemption, Thy Church, Thy Sacraments; in the Eucharist wherein Thou hast made a memorial of all Thy wonderful works. But most of all for Thy great glory, O Lord God, heavenly King, God the Father Almighty. O Lord Jesus Christ, the only-begotten Son. "Blessed art Thou, O Lord, our Father from eternity to eternity. Thine, O Lord, is magnificence, and power, and glory, and victory: and to Thee is praise: for all that is in heaven and in earth is Thine: Thine is the Kingdom, O Lord, and Thou art above all princes. Thine are riches, and Thine is glory; Thou hast dominion over all; in Thy hand is power and might; in Thy hand greatness and the empire of all things. Now, therefore, our God, we give thanks to Thee, and we praise Thy glorious name" (1 Par. 29:10-13).

Oblation & Petition, pp. 160, 162.

Prayer before a Crucifix, p. 12.

THE WELCOME OF A CREATURE

II

De profundis.

BEFORE COMMUNION

MY God, I wish that after Communion I could sink, sink, sink before Thee till I should reach that point of self-abasement which corresponds with the fundamental nothingness of the creature. That from this depth I might adore Thee, and that the recognition of the infinite distance between us might be accepted by Thy Divine Majesty as fitting adoration and praise. I unite myself with all those who, through the help of Thy Light, have reached that depth of lowliness. With the heavenly hierarchies, sinking lower and lower in Thy Presence as they are nobler, nearer to Thee, more loving, more beloved: with the sublime spirits who veil themselves before Thy Face: with the four-and-twenty ancients who cast their crowns at Thy feet: with that Handmaid of Thine who adores Thee from depths of abasement not given to us to sound or even conceive: with Thy Co-Eternal Son, very God of very God, who as Man annihilates Himself before Thee. From my place as a creature, in union with all creatures, I worship Thee, my God. *De profundis clamavi ad Te, Domine.*

Is there a lower depth than this? Can anything be beyond and beneath nothingness? Yes. That abyss if deep is not dark. It means infinite distance between the creature and the Creator, but the distance does not divide. On the contrary, it implies a relation, a drawing together by the correspondence between plenitude and need. But sin is black and repulsive, its final consequence utter and eternal separation of the Creator from the work of His hands.

What is sin? It is the practical denial of God's claims to our obedience. It is the deliberate turning against Him of the gifts we have received from His hand. And this while still clinging to that hand for life and the enjoyment of all life brings. This is what I have done when I sinned. This is that lower depth above which I see the level of simple creaturehood lying far above me, the sunlight of God's love upon it. *De profundis clamavi ad Te, Domine!*

There is yet another depth, the outcome of the other two—the depth of need. The creature's need is absolute. It has nothing of its own. Even the gift of itself is forever dependent on the Creator's Will. The natural life of its immortal spirit is indeed irrevocable in the sense that only by the same act of omnipotence that called it into being can it be withdrawn. But all that goes to make true life, life that deserves the name, the happiness that results from the full activity and satisfaction of all its powers—all this is the creature's need. It is the vast ocean bed that He who created it alone can fill. *Abyssus abyssum invocat. De profundis clamavi ad Te, Domine!*

But how can I fathom the need into which sin has plunged me? Of myself I have nothing, nothing wherewith to satisfy the cravings of my immortal soul. God is the End for which I was created, which I must attain, or pine for everlastingly in fruitless desire. And I have cut myself away from Him! What words can tell my need of that mercy which will bring Him once more within my reach! *Abyssus abyssum invocat. De profundis clamavi ad Te, Domine!*

After Communion

"O Lord, Lord, Almighty King, all things are in Thy power. Thou hast made heaven and earth and all things that are under the cope of heaven. Thou art Lord of all, and there is none that can resist Thy Majesty" (Esther 13:9-11).

Whence is this to me that my Lord should come to me?

Down, down, I sink in His Presence, like a speck floating through space from the most distant star. Down, down, till I reach the creature's place, the point whence it sprang from nothingness at the Creator's word. Oh that that depth were all! But deeper and darker than the void of nothingness is the abyss of sin. And into that depth His hand has reached—to save me. And to that misery His Heart has drawn Him—to love me. And to that degradation He has stooped—to raise me even to Himself.

"Give praise to our God, all ye His servants, and you that fear Him, little and great" (Apoc. 19:5).

"For He that is mighty hath done great things to me, and holy is His Name" (Luke 1:49).

"What shall I render to the Lord for all He hath rendered unto me? (Ps. 115:12).

"Bless the Lord, O my soul, and let all that is within me bless His holy Name. Bless the Lord, O my soul, and never forget all He hath done for thee" (Ps. 102:1-2).

"Praise ye the Lord from the heavens. Praise ye Him, all His Angels: praise ye Him, all His hosts" (Ps.148:1-2).

"Sing to Him, yea, sing praises to Him. Remember His marvelous works which He hath done" (Ps. 104:1,5).

"Give glory to the Lord for He is good; for His mercy endureth for ever" (Ps. 105:1).

De profundis. Terrible, my God, is the voice of sin going up discordant and defiant to the throne of Thy Majesty; going up at all hours—throughout the busy day, in the stillness of night. Yet I rejoice in the thought that it falls short, infinitely short, of the calm heights where in light inaccessible Thou dwellest, and no more troubles their serenity than the report or the smoke of our cannon perturbs the distant stars. I rejoice again in my littleness that limits my own power of offence. Thanks to my finite nature, I am not capable of an infinite act. Yet through the gift to me of Thyself I have control over what is infinite. Therefore my reparation can be greater than my wrong-doing. I have done evil before Thee, yet not with malice that is infinite. But with Christ in my heart I can give Thee infinite honour and glory. Thanks be to Thee for Thy unspeakable Gift! In atonement for my thanklessness I offer to Thee the praise of Thy well-beloved Son. In reparation for the indignity with which I have treated Thee, for all my irreverence in Thy Presence, I offer Thee Him who was heard for His reverence. In place of the service due to Thee, which, alas, I have so long withheld, I offer Thee the infinite value of His works who did always the things that please Thee. For all my coldness, my heedlessness and heartlessness towards Thee, my Creator and my Father, I offer Thee the infinite love of Thy dearly beloved Son, all the zeal of His service, all the labours and suffering of His life on earth, all His conformity with Thy Will that was the rule of His every thought, and word, and deed. Look upon the Face of Thy Christ, and look upon me in love and in pity for His sake.

Oblation & Petition, pp. 160, 162.

Prayer before a Crucifix, p. 12.

THE WELCOME OF A CHILD

THE WELCOME OF A CHILD

I

"Is not He thy Father that hath possessed thee, and made thee, and created thee?"—Deut. 32:6.

BEFORE COMMUNION

THERE, yonder, within the tabernacle that I could all but gird with my arms, is contained—*all that is;* the God of whom, by whom, in whom are all things; "the God of my life" (Ecclus. 23:4); "the God who has my breath in His hand" (Dan. 5:23).

And this God is my Father. To the tie that binds me to Him as His creature and servant He has superadded that of sonship. "Servant of God" is a title so grand and ennobling, that He Himself gives it to His special favourites: "My servant Abraham" (Gen. 26:24); "My servant Jacob" (Isa. 44:2); "My servant Moses" (Num. 12:7); "My servant Job"

(Job 42:7). Again and again He makes His promises affectionately "for the sake of My servant David" (3 Kings 11:32).

In the New Law, the Law of love, we find our Lord's chosen companions and friends glorying in the name of servants: "Simon Peter, servant and apostle of Jesus Christ"; "Paul, a servant of Jesus Christ." But this link was not close enough for the love of Him who gave us His only Son to be our Brother. "Behold what manner of charity the Father hath bestowed on us that we should be called and should be the sons of God" (1 John 3:1), cries out John, the beloved, the only one among the Apostles who in his Epistles does not call himself by the name of servant. "Dearly beloved, we are now the sons of God," he exclaims exultingly. "Therefore now we are not servants, but sons" (*idem*).

"Father" is the name put upon our lips by our Lord Himself. And it confers all that it signifies: "If sons, heirs also" (Gal. 4:7). It gives us a right to come before our Heavenly Father as "most dear children" (Eph. 5:1), to cry in all our needs: "Abba, Father!" The father is the bread-giver of the family. We cry to our Father in Heaven for our daily bread, for the food of the soul no less than for the food of the body. The cry of our heart is for Himself: "O God, my God, to Thee do I watch from the daybreak. For Thee my soul hath thirsted" (Ps. 62:2). "As the hart panteth for the water-brooks, so panteth my soul after Thee" (Ps. 41:2).

"And He gave them their desire; they were not defrauded of that which they craved...He gave them the Bread of heaven. Man ate the Bread of Angels" (Ps. 77:24-25). "Thou dost feed Thy people with the food of Angels, and gavest them bread from heaven prepared without labour, having in it all that is delicious, and the sweetness of every taste. For Thy sustenance showed Thy sweetness to Thy children... Thy children, O Lord, whom Thou lovest" (Wisd. 16:20-21;26).

A child preparing for First Communion said: "I think it's very wonderful that God should be our food; because, you know," she added hesitatingly, "He mightn't have liked it." Now and again there comes to us as to this child a momentary glimpse of the bewildering depth to which our God descends in this mystery. And then, like a flash of light, it is gone; and we look up to Him in the Host, and He comes to us at the altar-rails, and the veil is as thick as ever, and all we can do is to cry our "*Credo,*" and wait for the day when the reward of that "*Credo*" shall be the face-to-face Vision of Himself.

"This is God, our God" (Ps. 47:15). Not by the lightest unguarded step may love trench on reverence. But among the acts of reverence, the Infinite Majesty of God does not hold aloofness. We are at once creatures at the feet of our Creator, and royal children gathered round our Father's knee, treating familiarly with Him, carrying to Him all our needs, sporting in His presence, all the happier because His eye is upon us, because that eye sees the inmost heart. His own infinite perfection is His all-sufficing glory. He dispenses with the formalities of earthly courts and contents Himself with the simple homage of the lowliest of His subjects, the very youngest of His children.

My God, I am not surprised at many of the marvels faith teaches me concerning Thee—Thy Self-existence, Thy Eternity, Thy Omnipotence, Thy Infinitude in all perfection. But that Thou, Thine own Beatitude, shouldst be so enamoured of me, Thy little creature, this is incomprehensible, almost beyond belief. What joy that it is part of my belief, that this, among other mysteries, is included in my "*Credo;*" that coming trembling to unite myself to Thee, I hear Thee saying: "With desire I have desired."

Come, then, my Father—come to such a welcome as I can give Thee. Stoop indulgently to receive my worship, my thanksgiving, my loyalty, and my love.

AFTER COMMUNION

"Blessed be the Lord for this day" (3 Kings 5:7).

"Bless the Lord, O my soul, and never forget all He hath done for thee" (Ps. 102:2).

"Give praise to our God, all ye His servants, and you that fear Him, little and great" (Apoc. 19:5).

"Praise ye the Lord, for He is good; sing ye to His name, for it is sweet" (Ps. 134:3).

"For He hath satisfied the empty soul, and hath filled the hungry soul with good things" (Ps. 106:9).

"Thou art worthy, O Lord our God, to receive glory, and honour, and power" (Apoc. 4:11).

"Amen. Benediction, and glory, and wisdom, thanksgiving, honour, and power, and strength to our God for ever and ever. Amen" (Apoc. 7:12).

Oh, that I could at all realise the tremendous truth that I have in my heart as my own possession, my Creator and my Father; Him from whom I came; to whom I am returning; who holds in His hands my eternal destiny; with whom I have relations closer by far than those which link me with any creature!

A trusted servant, a confidant, a friend, a beloved child—all this I am to the God who made me. Have I not cause for the gladdest worship, for the willing tender of all I have and am, for offers of service that have no limit except such as my littleness and feebleness impose!

My God, who wouldst have me call Thee Father, teach me to reverence, love, and serve Thee as my Father. Put into my heart all Thou hast a right to expect from Thy child. Give me the high thoughts of the children of God, who set Thy glory and service before them as the goal of all their desires, who comport themselves at once as faithful servants and "most dear children." I earnestly desire to fulfill the first and greatest of Thy commandments—to love Thee with my whole heart and soul, with all my mind and with all my strength. Let me love Thee with my whole heart and soul by consecrating to Thee all my affections. Be first in my heart always. If I cannot love Thee with the ardour I shall some day, may I at least honour Thee by that love of preference that puts Thee and Thy rights before all other persons and claims. Let me love Thee with all my mind by tending to Thee in all my thoughts and works, directing them, not to any selfish end, but to the hallowing of Thy Name and the accomplishment of Thy Will in the duties of my state of life. Let me love Thee with all my strength, by persevering effort to bring my will into conformity with Thine, in spite of frailty and falls. Let me love, not in word and in tongue, but in deed and in truth. Make me relish hard work in Thy service, and be ready for personal inconvenience and sacrifice in Thy interests, the interests of the Church and of souls.

O my Father, when I come Home from my long journey, take me into Thy arms, and lay my head down on Thy breast, and make up to me for all the long absence from Thee, the weary groping after Thee, the fear of never reaching Thee, of which life has been full; for the distance between us caused by my sinfulness; for the miserable service of Thee that is partly my fault, and partly, O my Creator, the result of the frail nature Thy hands have made. As I lie there, folded fast to Thy breast, let my first nestling to Thee, my first happy tears, be to Thee the long-deferred adoration and thanksgiving and reparation and filial love, which in Thy Fatherly compassion Thou will account compensation for the past.

Oblation & Petition, pp. 160, 162.

Prayer before a Crucifix, p. 12.

THE WELCOME OF A CHILD

II

*"The same is my brother, and sister,
and mother"*—Matt. 12:50.

BEFORE COMMUNION

DEAREST to us among the attributes of our God is His Fatherhood. He cannot help being our Father: "Is not He thy Father, that hath possessed thee, and made thee, and created thee?" (Deut. 32:6). It is as our Father that we are to have recourse to Him. He is not merely the source of life and energy, a distant Governor, the Judge of the living and the dead. Not merely our Creator. But our true, loving, solicitous Father, who has made us by adoption what His only-begotten Son is by nature, "the sons of God," and co-heirs with Him who is the "First-born among many brethren."

Yet even this loving name of Father does not exhaust our claims upon His love. He tells us to think of Him in all manner of incompatible relations, as lover, brother, sister, mother. "Thou hast wounded My Heart, My sister, My spouse" (Cant. 4:9). "Whosoever shall do the Will of My Father that is in Heaven, he is My brother, and sister, and mother."

Each of these relations implies a peculiar and distinct love, and all are found united in Him. There is the love of a brother, devoted, cherishing, protecting; the mother's love, vigilant, self-sacrificing, indulgent, with a boundless compassion for every weakness and misfortune; the love of sister and of spouse, with their special characteristics and sweetness—all that is beautiful in human love, intensified to an inconceivable degree.

What is there in me to attract love such as this? Nay, rather, how is it that even such consuming love as Thine, O Lord, is not extinguished by contact with my frozen heart? St. Teresa was willing that others should be above her in glory, but she did not think she could be content to know that any one loved Thee more than she did. A quite contrary desire would become me. Knowing the wretchedness of my love and service, I ought by rights to wish that every creature of Thine should love Thee more than I. And yet,

Lord, I cannot desire this. I could not bear that the multitudes who have received less, immeasurably less from Thy hand than I have, should love Thee more. At least I cannot bear to be the last and lowest in the ranks of those who love Thee. Rather will I entreat Thee, who canst do all things, to make my dull, cold heart more like that glowing heart of Teresa. It caught its flame from Thine. And Thou art coming to me now. Take my heart, inflame it by contact with Thine own, O God, who art a consuming fire.

After Communion

"Holy, Holy, Holy, Lord God of hosts."

"Let all the earth adore Thee and sing to Thee" (Ps. 65:4).

"Let all Thy Angels and Saints bless Thee, and praise Thee, and glorify Thee for ever" (Dan. 3).

"What shall I render to the Lord for all that He hath rendered to me?" (Ps. 115:12).

"Let all Thy works, O Lord, praise Thee, and let all Thy Saints bless Thee" (Ps. 144:10).

My God, Thou art with me, and I am cold, and hard, and dry. As far as this comes of my want of faith, of appreciation of the honour Thou dost me, and of the love Thou showest me, I deplore it with all my heart. But inasmuch as it is a just punishment of my sins, a satisfaction that I may make for them, a pain I can bear for Thee, I resign myself to it heartily. I have no right to the children's bread; the smallest crumbs, the driest crusts are more than I deserve.

O Infinite Love that comest to me, and comest willingly in spite of my unworthiness, no coldness, nor hardness, nor sense of punishment, nor pain, shall hinder me from presenting myself before Thee to offer Thee, just as it is, this poor heart of mine which Thou hast come so far to seek.

I trust Thee, my God, to bring victory out of weakness, peace at last out of a long and weary fight, the realisation of Thy designs out of my mistakes and my sinfulness.

What is there, my Father and best of friends, that I shall fear to trust to Thee?

My past? I am sorry for everything in it that has displeased or even disappointed Thee. I know that I have sinned against Thee. But Thy dearly beloved Son offers Himself daily for me in the Mass, a Victim able to cancel the sins of a thousand worlds, and in Holy Communion He helps me again and again to make my acts of contrition.

My present? I know that my daily sins and infidelities may well make Thee turn away Thy face from me. But in the Holy Sacrifice and in my Communions I offer Thee a full satisfaction for all my shortcomings.

My future? Oh no, my Father, to whom could I trust it but to Thee! I know that I have cause to fear Thy judgments, and I do fear them, else should I not be safe. But my trust is greater than my fear, for my fear is based on myself, but my trust on Thee.

Look then, O Lord, upon the face of Thy Christ, who has given Himself a redemption for me, and in my Father's house has prepared a place for me. Look on Thy beloved Son in whom Thou art well pleased, and for His sake look on me with pity and with love. Not only forgive the past and the present, but give so abundantly in the future, that before my death I may have made good all my losses, and satisfied Thee, my God!

Oblation & Petition, p. 10.

Prayer before a Crucifix, p. 12.

THE WELCOME OF A
SINNER

THE WELCOME OF A SINNER

I

"I am not come to call the just, but sinners"—Matt. 9:13.

66 WHY doth your Master eat and drink with publicans and sinners?" said the Scribes and Pharisees to the Twelve, when at Matthew's feast "many publicans and sinners sat down together with Jesus and His disciples. And Jesus hearing this, said: They that are in health need not a physician, but they that are ill…I am not come to call the just, but sinners."

Notice how quickly our Lord makes reply. He answers Himself, not only to free His disciples from a difficulty, but because He willed that no lips but His own should give the reply to a question that so nearly concerns each one of us, a question that gave Him an opportunity of showing His love for the outcast and the despised, and of drawing them to Himself by words more winning than any that the most tender of His servants could have framed.

He did not repudiate the charge of being the Friend of publicans and sinners. On the contrary, He welcomed it. The cavillers did Him a service who made it a reproach and spread it far and wide. It was no calumny, but a blessed truth, and He had nothing more at heart than to see it credited by every human heart that had gone astray.

Do not Thy predilections, O Lord, refute our arguments for abstaining from Communion on the ground of our unworthiness? Thou hast not changed since the days of Thy life on earth. Thy pleasure still is to be among the sinful and the weak. Should they not flock around Thee now as then; now as then "make haste and receive Thee with joy?"

O God, it is hard at times not to despair of my heart! If only Thou hadst not done so much for me; or if the Incarnation and the Eucharist were wonders wrought for mankind in general and not for me individually, with special reference to my needs, out of a personal love of me! Or if Thou wert less patient and forbearing! But, knowing Thee by experience to be what Thou art, how can I offend thee as I do and feel it so little? It is not that I do not love Thee, my

God; Thou knowest that I love Thee. Yet where are the signs that, when love is present, betray it on every side? My heart ought to be broken when I think of my sins. It should overflow in praise and thanksgiving at the sight of all Thou hast done and daily dost for me. It should be wrung with sorrow at the sight of outrages committed against Thee. It ought to pant with desire when I think of the hour when I shall appear before Thy face and see Thee as Thou art.

My God, had I the power over my heart which Thou hast, things, I think, would be different. Yet there must be a good side to this humiliating state if, being able to work a change, Thou leavest me as I am. There may be more true worship as I kneel cold and mute at Thy feet, than if I had all the sensible fervour I desire. And if this poor service satisfies Thee and is safer for me, I will be content to remain thus as long as Thou wilt, solicitous for one thing only—that this sense of distance from Thee shall not be due to conscious fault of mine.

After Communion

"I am the Lord your Holy One" (Isa. 43:15).

O great and holy God, I bow myself down in the dust before Thee. With the veiled Seraphim I adore Thee: Holy, Holy, Holy, Lord God of hosts. "O Lord my God, my Holy One" (Hab. 1:12), how canst Thou come to me? How canst Thou bear union such as this with a soul like mine? With the centurion I confess: "Lord, I am not worthy that Thou shouldst come under my roof." With Peter I ought to cry out: "Depart from me, O Lord, for I am a sinner." Yet I shall please Thee better if, with the disciples at Emmaus, I entreat Thee: "Stay with me, stay with me, O Lord!" It is by Thine own invitation that I have drawn near to Thee: "Come to Me all you that labour and are heavy burdened." I may come, for I have a burden to lay at Thy feet. I may come, for Thy invitation is to all.

I am sorry for whatever displeases Thee in my soul. I am sorry, not so much for any pain or hurt to myself that sin has brought, as for its outrage to Thy holiness. Wash me from my iniquity and cleanse me from my sin. "For Thou, O Lord, art sweet and mild, a God of compassion, patient, and of much mercy, and true" (Ps. 85:5,15). Thou hast come to me today as my Food, that I may taste and see that the Lord is sweet.

O sweetest Lord, remember that Thou hast come to call and draw to Thyself such as I am. Remember that if Thine eyes have seen sin in my soul, they have seen sorrow too. Remember that a contrite and humble heart Thou hast never despised.

"I have gone astray like a sheep that is lost; seek Thy servant" (Ps. 118:176).

"Behold I Myself will seek My sheep, and will visit them. As the shepherd visiteth his flock, so will I visit My sheep, and will deliver them out of all the places where they have been scattered in the cloudy and dark day. I will feed them in the most fruitful pastures; there they shall rest on the green grass; I will feed My sheep; and I will cause them to lie down, saith the Lord God. I will seek that which was lost; and that which was driven away, I will bring again; and I will bind up that which was broken, and I will strengthen that which was weak, and that which was fat and strong I will preserve" (Ezech. 34:11,12,14,15,16).

O Shepherd of my soul, what thanks shall I give Thee for having sought me so long and so unweariedly! Thou hast brought me out of the places where I was lost in the cloudy and dark day. Thou hast fed me with sweetest pasturage. Thou wilt have me to trust to Thee all my concerns, both spiritual and temporal, to cast all my care on Thee, resting in peace in the keeping of Thy Providence. And still I am afraid. That which was driven away Thou hast brought back to Thee. But, O my Shepherd, I am wounded, I am weak. How shall my future be better than my past? "I am Thine, save me." (Ps. 118:94). The resolutions so often broken I entrust to Thee. Let me find by experience that I can do all things in Him who strengthens me. Let me say in my gratitude and my joy: "The Lord is good to them that hope in Him" (Lam. 3:25). "The Lord is good, and giveth strength in the day of trouble" (Nahum 1:7). "How great is the mercy of the Lord, and His forgiveness to them that turn to Him!" (Ecclus. 17:28).

Oblation & Petition, p. 82.

Prayer before a Crucifix, p. 12.

THE WELCOME OF A SINNER

II

"Thy faith hath made thee safe"—Luke 7:50.

"AND behold a woman that was in the city, a sinner, when she knew that He sat at meat in the Pharisee's house, brought an alabaster box of ointment. And, standing behind at His feet, she began to wash His feet with tears, and wiped them with the hairs of her head, and kissed His feet, and anointed them with the ointment."

She came before Him unbidden. The invitation: "Come to Me all you that labour," had not yet been given. She had not heard that "they that are well need not the physician, but they that are sick"; that He had "not come to call the just, but sinners"; that there is "joy before the Angels of God upon one sinner doing penance." Would it not be rashness no less than irreverence to thrust herself upon His notice? Her presence might be as offensive to Him as it was sure to be to His host and the guests. Should she not wait a fitter opportunity, seek first an intercessor to plead her cause, secure at least His approval for such an intrusion?

No, she could not wait; she could not reason. Reckless of results, she hurried to her salvation as she had hurried to her ruin. Her need drove her to Him. Her need was her counsellor and her defense. She had seen Him, and seeing Him had seen herself. Careless and curious, she had penetrated one day the crowd that followed Him. She had met His eye. She had cowered before it. The consciousness of her sin had been burnt into her by that glance. She had become intolerable to herself: what must she be to Him! And yet, how was it that that look had not repelled her? Her instinct was, not to hide away out of His sight, but to fly to Him, the All-Holy, and trust herself to Him. No misgivings deterred her; no humiliation affrighted her; she had seen Him; His eye had rested on her— what was all the world to her now?

And He said to her: "Thy sins are forgiven thee. Thy faith hath made thee safe. Go in peace."

How complete was Magdalen's faith in Him! She made her plans without a thought of interference or repulse. She took her costly ointment and went straight to His feet, and washed, and kissed, and anointed them. Who among His chosen friends, the privileged, the innocent, would have dared what she dared that day!

O happy penitent, so sure of acceptance and of mercy that thou neededst not to plead in words, but only with those tears that were at once sorrow, and reparation, and love!

Truly, O Lord, she is an Apostle. She has preached Thee throughout the world with a persuasiveness that is all her own. She has brought Thee more converts than the most intrepid, the most zealous of missioners. For she has revealed to all ages the far-reaching mercy of Thy Human Heart. Only when the secrets of all hearts are disclosed will be known the multitudes that, but for Mary Magdalen, had been lost to Thee for ever. But with her they crept to Thy feet; with her they washed them with their tears. And for them also were the blessed words: "Thy sins are forgiven thee. Go in peace."

I, a sinner, am drawing near to Thee now. Oh that it might be with her faith and trust, with her contrition and her tears! I offer Thee the dispositions which made her so acceptable to Thee. Give me a share in them, that I too, cleansed from all stain, may become dear and precious in Thy sight.

AFTER COMMUNION

O God, all Holy, I bow myself down before Thee. In my sinfulness I have drawn near to Thee like Magdalen, nearer than she was when she knelt at Thy feet. I have no tears for my sins, no ointment, no kiss. My heart is dry and cold, without love; almost, as it seems to me, without faith. But I have desires, and these are acceptable to Thee. And I may bring to Thee as my own the treasures which by the Communion of Saints I share. I thank and bless and praise Thee with all the Angels of heaven who rejoice over every sinner that doth penance. I offer Thee the adoration and thanksgiving of all the Blessed, of those in particular to whom much has been forgiven; the adoration and the love of Magdalen; the gratitude with which she recalls the day when, with her many sins upon her, she hastened to Thy feet. I offer to Thee the joy Thou wilt have in her throughout eternity. Receive, dear Lord, another sinner now. Give me, to whom many sins have been forgiven, the grace to love much. And let my love and my thanksgiving be a joy to Thee for ever.

Magdalen never doubted her forgiveness. I will never doubt mine. She heard her absolution from Thine own lips. I from the lips of Thy Church hear the blessed words: "I absolve thee; go in peace." And on Thy word that what the Church looses on earth is loosed in heaven, I believe.

Magdalen never forgot that many sins had been forgiven her. She did not account an absolution, even such as hers, exemption from the obligation of doing penance. Thenceforth her life was one of penance, but a penance penetrated through and through with joy, and sweetened by the contrite love that seeks an outlet in reparation.

Magdalen was faithful to the end. She stood firm when even Apostles faltered. She clung to her Lord in disgrace. She shared His shame. She sought Him perseveringly when He hid Himself from her. She carried His messages to the wavering and the sorrowful. She stayed the faith of the less fervent on her own. And when He had left the earth she followed Him in desire, and through years of persevering penance kept her heart for Him.

Let me be like her, O Lord. Let me remember that though sin is forgiven, the obligation of penance remains. Let me take from Thy hand in the spirit of penance my daily crosses, the weariness and

disappointments of life, all that it costs to struggle
with self, to sacrifice self for the sake of others—that
is, for Thy sake, my God. Let me, like blessed Mary
Magdalen, be a messenger of Thine to those among
whom I live, making Thy service easier for them and
happier. Let me, like Magdalen, be faithful to Thee
to the end, and be with her through eternity among
the happy ones who have put their trust in Thee and
not been confounded.

Oblation & Petition, pp. 160, 162.

Prayer before a Crucifix, p. 12.

THE WELCOME OF PRAISE

THE WELCOME OF PRAISE

I

"Give praise to our God, all ye His servants, and you that fear Him, little and great"—Apoc. 19:5.

BEFORE COMMUNION

OUR needs are so many and so pressing that they well-nigh absorb all our thoughts and all the energies of our souls when we go to pray. We come to think of prayer as if it were petition only, losing sight of that highest, purest prayer, the only prayer that is to endure throughout eternity—*praise*. We know, of course, that it is our duty to praise God here on earth, but the rush of life and its innumerable calls upon our interest and our time, make us apt to lose sight of our obligation. We find it hard to rise above our daily cares to the refreshing heights where earth and its passing concerns are left behind, and we breathe the pure air of heaven; where, with Angels and Archangels, and with all the heavenly army, we may sing: "Holy, Holy, Holy, Lord God of hosts; heaven and earth are full of Thy glory. Hosanna in the highest."

Therefore the Church is ever saying to us : "*Sursum corda!*" Every day she bids her priests and religious set aside for awhile the prayer of supplication, and lift up their voices to heaven in a chorus of pure praise. And in the *Gloria in excelsis* and the *Gloria Patri* she would have us one and all sing Lauds to God and practice the eternal Alleluia.

This praise is not so hard as we imagine, or God would not have made it the first of our duties. We excuse ourselves, perhaps, by saying we cannot sing the song of the Lord in a strange land. Were we unfallen still, it would come as readily to our lips as to those of Adam and Eve in Paradise. But when earth has become an exile, and we wake each morning to toil and trouble, we have neither motive nor heart for praise.

Yet men and women, burdened like ourselves, have soared above these things. Nay, more, they have made this elevation of heart an exercise that habit has rendered easy and delightful, and have found in it a resource and a refuge in the trials of life. Why should not we do the like? We turn out for our

constitutional in all weathers, often enough sorely
against our inclination. The body pleads fatigue,
indisposition, business as an excuse. But in the very
interests of health and work, we drive it from the
fireside out on to the moors or the hillside. If we
would use the same resolution in behalf of the self-
concentred spirit, and raise it, perforce, into a rarer,
more bracing atmosphere, we should find that even
in our own interests God has laid it upon us as a duty
to lift up our hearts to Him in praise.

How differently people look at things!

"'Blessed be His most Sacred Heart' has been
added to the prayers after Mass," grumbled some.
"The Pope seems to think we have nothing to do
but pray."

"I am so glad we have another Divine Praise,"
wrote a little schoolboy to his mother.

Again, praise is not so hard as we suppose, because
our soul is an instrument attuned to the note of
praise. To praise is the very motive of its existence.
The spontaneity and facility with which it yields its
admiration to the passing beauties of earth, speaks of
an instinct heaven-born. What should it be when the
object of its contemplation is the Creator Himself!

Whatever is grand or winning, strong or tender, wise or sweet in nature, grace, or glory, is of Him and from Him. Hence, we are surrounded on every side by incentives to praise. The manifestation of His perfections is so varied and so marvellous, that it must appeal to all who have eyes to see, and ears to hear.

Are we attracted by majesty and glory and power? "Who shall search out His glorious acts. And who shall show forth the power of His majesty?" (Ecclus. 18:3-4). Do we bow down before beauty and holiness? "The Lord is clothed with beauty" (Ps.92:1). "O Lord my God, Thou hast put on praise and beauty, and art clothed with light as with a garment" (Ps.103:1-2). "Who is like to Thee, glorious in holiness?" (Ex. 15:11). If we seek love, goodness, fidelity, mercy, all these are found in our God as in their source. "God is love" (1 John 4:16). "One is good—God" (Matt. 19:17). He is the "Faithful and True" (Apoc. 19: 11). "And who shall be able to declare His mercy?" (Ecclus. 18:4). "Give glory to the Lord, for He is good; for His mercy endureth for ever. Let them say so that have been redeemed by the Lord, whom He hath redeemed from the hand of the enemy. Let the mercies of the Lord give glory to Him, and His wonderful works to the children of men" (Ps. 106:8).

Is there any conceivable good that is not found in our God? And does not the secret history of our own life bear testimony to His mercy, His fidelity, His love? Why, then, should not our hearts leap up to him in praise?

How He must desire our praise when He permits it to mingle with that of the blessed spirits before His throne; when He discloses to us even here the mysteries of that kingdom where there are secret words not given to man to utter! We hear the adoring praise of the four living creatures that rest not day and night, saying: "Holy, Holy, Holy." And of the four-and-twenty Ancients that cast their crowns before the throne, saying: "Thou art worthy, O Lord our God, to receive glory, and honour, and power." And of the great multitude, that no man can number, that cry with a loud voice: "Salvation to our God who sitteth on the throne, and to the Lamb." And not only do we hear, but we are invited to join. The Communion of Saints is not a beautiful dream, but a sweet reality. And, therefore, with Angels and Archangels, with Thrones and Dominations, and with all the host of heaven, we sing a hymn to His glory, saying: "Holy, Holy, Holy, Lord God of hosts; heaven and earth are full of Thy glory. Hosanna in the highest!"

The Blessed do not disdain our companionship. How should they? Our Lord is theirs. He whom they adore with veiled faces has bid us call Him "Father." Therefore our voices are admitted with theirs in suppliant praise.

"God doth great things and unsearchable, and wonderful things without number" (Job 5:9). He is wonderful in His Saints, in His Church, in His Sacraments, in His mysteries. But most of all in that Sacrament of Sacraments, in that Mystery of faith, in which "He hath made a remembrance of all His wonderful works" (Ps. 110:4). It is before and after Communion that praise is truly meet and just, easiest, and most acceptable. Because then our praise is not alone. By Him, and with Him, and in Him, it rises to the Father. After Communion that becomes possible which might have seemed impossible—to give to God a worship that is commensurate with all His claims upon us; that covers His perfections with a co-extensive and perfectly adequate praise. Will not admiration, loyalty, gratitude, exult during the quarter of an hour of thanksgiving? And even if they seem cold and dull—what of that! He is with us, He is given to us whose praise alone suffices. "Thanks be to God for His Unspeakable Gift!"

AFTER COMMUNION

"Blessed be the Lord God this day" (3 Kings 5:7).

"Every day will I bless Thee: and I will praise Thy name for ever, yea for ever and ever. Great is the Lord, and greatly to be praised; and of His greatness there is no end" (Ps. 144:2-3).

"Praise the Lord, O my soul; I will praise the Lord, I will sing to my God as long as I shall be" (Ps. 145:2).

"To Him that sitteth on the throne, and to the Lamb, benediction, and honour, and glory, and power, for ever and ever. Amen" (Apoc. 5:13).

"Salvation to our God who sitteth upon the throne, and to the Lamb. Amen. Benediction, and glory, and wisdom, and thanksgiving, honour, and power, and strength to our God for ever and ever. Amen" (Apoc. 7:10,12).

"Give praise to our God, all ye His servants, and you that fear Him, little and great" (Apoc. 19:5).

"Give glory to the Lord, for He is good; for His mercy endureth for ever" (Ps. 106:1).

Laudetur Jesus Christus!

For the eternal counsel which decreed that the Word should be made Flesh and dwell amongst us,

May Jesus Christ be praised!

For the love with which "Christ loved us and delivered Himself for us" (Eph. 5:2),

> *May Jesus Christ be praised!*

For the love with which "He loved me and delivered Himself for me" (Gal. 2:20),

> *May Jesus Christ be praised!*

For the love with which He became to us "as a neighbour and as an own brother" (Ps. 34:14),

> *May Jesus Christ be praised!*

For the sufferings of His infancy, the privations of His childhood, the hardships of His youth, the toils and journeyings of His manhood,

> *May Jesus Christ be praised!*

For His holy and gentle teaching when "He spake as never man spake" (John vii.),

> *May Jesus Christ be praised!*

For His miracles of mercy, when He showed Himself to us "gracious and full of compassion" (2 Esdras 9:17),

> *May Jesus Christ be praised!*

For the love with which He made Himself "like to us in all things without sin" (Heb. 4:15),

> *May Jesus Christ be praised!*

For the love with which "He was wounded for our iniquities and bruised for our sins" (Isa. 53:5),

> *May Jesus Christ be praised!*

For the love with which He "bought us with a great price" (1 Cor. 6:20),

> *May Jesus Christ be praised!*

For the love with which He "washed us from our sins in His own blood" (Apoc. 1:5),

> *May Jesus Christ be praised!*

For the love with which "He has redeemed us to God in His Blood, out of every tribe, and tongue, and people, and nation" (Apoc. 5:9),

> *May Jesus Christ be praised!*

For the love with which "He was delivered up for our sins and rose again for our justification" (Rom. 4:25),

> *May Jesus Christ be praised!*

For the love with which He ascended into Heaven "to prepare a place for us" (John 14:2),

> *May Jesus Christ be praised!*

For the "Unspeakable Gift" of His abiding Presence whereby He is "with us all days, even to the consummation of the world" (Matt, 28:20),

> *May Jesus Christ be praised!*

For His coming to me today that I may live by Him, and have everlasting life, and be raised up by Him at the Last Day,

> *May Jesus Christ be praised!*

By the perfections of His Sacred Manhood and the infinite dignity of His Divine Person,

May Jesus Christ be praised!

By Mary, handmaid of the Lord, and Mother of God, in whom His Redemption hath a perfect work,

May Jesus Christ be praised!

By the four-and-twenty Ancients, and the four living creatures who "fall down before the Lamb" (Apoc. 4:10),

May Jesus Christ be praised!

By Angels and Archangels, and all the host of Heaven,

May Jesus Christ be praised!

By the hundred and forty-four thousand who "follow Him whithersoever He goeth" (Apoc. 14:4),

May Jesus Christ be praised!

By Patriarchs and Prophets, by Apostles and Martyrs, by Confessors and Virgins,

May Jesus Christ be praised!

By the "great multitude which no man could number, of all nations and tribes, and peoples, and tongues," standing before the throne and in sight of the Lamb (Apoc. 7:9),

May Jesus Christ be praised!

By this soul of mine with all its faculties; by my body with all its senses; by every aspiration of my mind and every affection of my heart; by my every thought, and word, and act, in time and in eternity,

    May Jesus Christ be praised!

By all who are near and dear to me, all entrusted to me, all who are bound to me by the ties of kindred or of friendship,

    May Jesus Christ be praised!

By all who are gathered together in the One fold of the One Shepherd,

    May Jesus Christ be praised!

By His other sheep whom He has yet to bring into His fold,

    May Jesus Christ be praised!

By those who are still wandering afar off in the shadow of death,

    May Jesus Christ be praised!

By every creature His hand hath made,

    May Jesus Christ be praised!

Oblation and Petition

What is there, Lord, that Thou hast not sacrificed for my sake? Thou hast given Thy body to the strikers, Thy face to them that smote it and spit upon it, Thy head to the thorns, Thy hands and feet to the nails, Thy Heart to the lance. Thou hast parted with reputation; Thou hast borne treason, ingratitude, the abandonment of friends, the dereliction of God; Thou hast made over to me Thy merits, Thy Mother, Thy Kingdom, Thy very Self in the Eucharist. Truly mayst Thou ask: "What is there that I ought to have done for My vineyard that I have not done?"

I thank Thee, O dearest Lord, for all Thou hast suffered for me, and for the love with which Thou hast suffered. For all Thou hast given me, and for the love with which it has been given. I thank Thee for all Thou art to me, for all Thou wilt be to me in eternity. Happy those who during this short life have made Thee some return for Thy devotedness, and returned Thee love for love. What have I given Thee up to now? What return am I going to make—not by delegates, but by myself—a personal return for a personal gift?

I offer Thee, O Lord, the joy Thou wilt have today in the Communions of those who love Thee best. I cannot hope to be counted among these happy souls, but by the Communion of Saints I share in the treasures that make their hearts so pleasing to Thee. I share in their love, in their thanksgiving, in the welcome they will give Thee, I offer Thee all this as if it were my own.

I offer Thee what is in very deed my own—my poverty, my wretchedness, my nothingness, and the humiliation that comes of so much misery. I offer Thee the daily work and trials and cares of my life. I commend to Thee the unforeseen occasions in which I shall need the special assistance of Thy grace; and the opportunities I may have of helping others. I unite all I shall do or suffer, all I shall think or say, with Thy thoughts and words and actions whilst on earth. I thank Thee for every joy Thou hast in store for me. I accept of every trial. I accept of death in the form and at the hour Thou shalt appoint. I accept Thy judgment of me when I shall stand before Thee to give an account of my poor, sinful life, and of the stewardship confided to me. I accept the eternity which will then begin for me. And if I had anything further, anything more precious to offer Thee and to trust to Thee, I would lay it all here at Thy feet.

Prayer before a Crucifix, p. 12.

THE WELCOME OF PRAISE

II

"Bless the Lord, O my soul, and let all that is within me bless His holy Name"—Ps. 102:1.

Before Communion

66 **B**LESS the Lord." Thus it ought to be, but what is the fact? Ah, Lord, Thou knowest. "My soul is as earth without water unto Thee" (Ps. 142:6). Hard and immovable as a rock, cold as ice, heavy as lead, I can do nothing, feel nothing, but the weight of my insensibility and my misery. I can grieve for any sin or infidelity that may be the cause of this callousness, but I can do nothing to remove it. Effort would be worse than useless. Better to lie still at Thy feet, content with a state of suffering that, after all, is not sin, trying and humiliating enough for me, but not necessarily displeasing to Thee. And if not,

why should I be disturbed? *Quare tristis es anima mea?* Why art thou sad, my soul, and why dost thou trouble me? Hope in God, for I will still give praise to Him. My very powerlessness praises Him; praises His almightiness, in such contrast to my feebleness; praises His goodness in coming to my wretchedness; His love that puts up with my coldness and takes me into its embrace just as I am.

"Bless God at all times" (Tobias 4:20). Yes, Lord, this is my desire, even when words of blessing come grudgingly and slow. "With my will, I will give praise to Him," says David (Ps. 27:7). Not a word about feelings. Thou dost not require them; why should I make myself unhappy about them?

These are times that, with all their pain, are not without consolation. It is something to entertain so great a Majesty at my own cost. And if Thou art content, I must needs be so too. Only see that my state involves no displeasure or dishonour to Thee, and I will bear it patiently—nay, joyfully. For all this will pass. The hiding of Thy face, the distress of my irresponsiveness will end with this life. In a little while I shall see Thee as Thou art; my soul shall magnify Thee even as I desire. "I shall be satisfied when Thy glory shall appear" (Ps. 16:15).

My God, I offer Thee that praise of mine when I pass within the eternal gates, and, swift as light, wing my way to Thy Throne. When the sight of Thee as Thou art shall set my soul free to pour itself out to Thee in one delighted, irrepressible, unending burst of song. When there shall be no more dullness and heaviness to clog the flight of my affections, no more selfishness to absorb what is Thine by right. But like the lark in the high heavens carolling to the Sun, my whole being shall go out to Thee in a jubilee of praise.

Meantime, what can I offer Thee, my God? Have I nothing, literally nothing by which I may at least testify my good will? A good will is fertile in expedients, and finds means even in obstacles. What can I find in my poverty that may be made available for praise? A callousness that cannot be stirred, a stupidity and hardness absolutely impenetrable— can this be material for praise? Yes, even this. For it can glorify the Creator by witnessing to the misery and indigence of the creature. It can be the humbly recognised chastisement of sin, an offering always acceptable to Thee. It can intensify the contrast between the all-mighty, all-eager Lover, and the poor, crippled creature that cannot lift itself to meet Him or make any response to His advances. My God, I

offer Thee this glory and this praise. I offer it gladly.
It is of my own stock, my own furnishing. But for
me, Thou couldst not have it. Accept it from me, O
Lover, as a pledge of what I would give were I able,
what I will give some day. My soul is as earth without
water to Thee, now. But the day will come when
"the land that was desolate shall be glad, and the
wilderness shall rejoice and shall flourish as the lily. It
shall bud forth and blossom, and shall rejoice with joy
and praise" (Isa. 35:1-2).

AFTER COMMUNION

"Thou art worthy, O Lord our God, to receive
glory, and honour, and power" (Apoc. 4:11).

"Let all Thy Angels and Saints bless Thee, and
praise Thee, and glorify Thee for ever" (Dan. 3:58).

"Let all the earth adore Thee and sing to Thee"
(Ps. 65:4).

"Let all Thy works, O Lord, praise Thee, and let
Thy Saints bless Thee" (Ps. 144:10).

"Sing praises to our God, sing ye; sing praises to
our King, sing ye" (Ps. 46:7).

"It is good to give praise to the Lord, and to sing to
Thy Name, O Most High" (Ps. 91:2).

"Praise the Lord, O my soul; I will praise the Lord,
I will sing to my God as long as I shall be" (Ps. 145:2).

"Laudamus Te, benedicimus Te, adoramus Te, glorificamus Te!" We praise Thee; we bless Thee; we adore Thee; we glorify Thee.

Laudamus Te! My God, I praise Thee for Thyself. What I conceive as Thy Perfections are in reality Thy Nature, Thy very Essence. Thou art not omnipotent, wise, truthful, beautiful, loving, good; but Omnipotence, Wisdom, Truth, Beauty, Goodness, Love. I praise Thee, then, for what is worthy of infinite praise. Were I capable of this, nothing less would be due to Thee from me. And, thanks be to Thee, I am capable now when Thy dearly beloved Son is with me, praising Thee with all the might and the love of His Sacred Human Soul. I unite my praise with His. By Him, with Him, in Him, in union with all Angels and Saints who praise Thee through Him, I lift up my voice to Thee in praise.

Benedicimus Te! My God, I bless Thee for all Thou art to us; for Thy eternal love of us; for all Thou hast wrought for us in time. I bless Thee for the Incarnation and Life, the Death and Resurrection of Thy beloved Son. I bless Thee for giving us His Mother and His Church; for all the Sacraments, especially for that which is by pre-eminence the Blessed Sacrament; and for that other without which the Eucharist would be a Gift beyond our reach—

the dear Sacrament of reconciliation and of peace. I bless Thee, my God, for all Thou art to me, for all that out of Thy treasury Thou hast bestowed upon me—for life, and time, and grace; for the gifts of mind and body given or withheld according to Thy knowledge of my need and Thy designs for my eternal happiness. I bless Thee for all Thy graces and favours bestowed upon me through the Mass, and in the Sacraments, and by the means of prayer. I bless Thee for Thy untiring patience with me and Thy forgiveness of my many sins; for Thy visits to me in Holy Communion; for Thy help in need; for the inspirations and invitations by which Thou seekest to draw me to Thyself, I bless Thee for the joys and for the trials of my life which in Thy Providence work together for my good. I bless Thee for the grace of final perseverance in Thy service, for Thy merciful judgment of my poor, sinful life; for the place in Thy kingdom to which Thou wilt bring me when my term of purification is past; for the joy of standing in Thy Presence for ever, and the sight of Thy unveiled Face. "Every day will I bless Thee: and I will praise Thy name for ever, yea for ever and ever" (Ps. 144:2).

Adoramus Te! My God, I adore Thee. I have but the faintest idea now of that worship, that self-annihilation that is the soul's response to the sight of Thy holiness, Thy majesty, Thy beauty, Thy power. But present within me is the Soul of Christ that comprehends Thy Divine Majesty fully, and is able to give Thee an adequate adoration. To its worship I unite mine. Through Him, and with Him, and in Him is to Thee, O God the Father, in the unity of the Holy Ghost, all honour and glory, world without end. Amen.

Glorificamus Te! My God, I glorify Thee for all Thou art in Thyself, and for all the manifestations of Thyself in nature, grace, and glory. The irrational creatures glorify Thee by doing Thy Will. The heavens declare the glory of God, the earth and sea lift up their voice to Thee in praise. Oh, that all men would glorify Thee! That they would all respond to the summons: "Give glory to God, all ye His servants, and you that fear Him, little and great" (Apoc. 19:5). "Glorify the Lord as much as ever you can, for He will yet far exceed, and His magnificence is wonderful. Blessing the Lord, exalt Him as much as you can, for He is above all praise" (Ecclus. 43:32-33). Yet after Communion I, a little one indeed, can glorify Him sufficiently. His boundless Perfections will not outstrip my praise. I may cover them with an infinite worship. I may exalt them as much as they deserve. For I can

do all things in Him who strengthens me then. Not I,
but my Lord and God with me. By Him, with Him,
in Him, is to God the Father, in the unity of the Holy
Ghost, all honour and glory, world without end.

Oblation and Petition, p. 10.

Prayer before a Crucifix, p. 12.

THE WELCOME OF A FRIEND

THE WELCOME OF A FRIEND

I

"Who art Thou, Lord?"

SAUL was on his way to Damascus to bring bound to Jerusalem the disciples of Christ, when "suddenly a light from heaven shined round about him." And falling on the ground he heard a voice saying to him: "Saul, Saul, why persecutest thou Me?" Who said: "Who art Thou, Lord?"

What a contrast between "Saul breathing out threatening and slaughter against the disciples of the Lord," and Paul who counted as nothing "perils of waters, perils of robbers, stripes, stoning, hunger and thirst, cold and nakedness," death itself for Jesus' sake; between the neophyte crying out in his ignorance: "Who art Thou, Lord?" and the Apostle exclaiming: "I know whom I have believed."

What had brought about this marvellous change? One thing: St. Paul had come to know our Lord—to know Him intimately, as one friend knows another. And because he knew Him, he had come to love Him with so vehement an affection that he could say: "Who shall separate us from the love of Christ? Shall tribulation, or danger, or the sword? I am sure that neither death nor life, nor things present, nor things to come, nor any creature, shall be able to separate us from the love of God which is in Christ Jesus our Lord."

How had St. Paul learned to know our Lord so well? He was not one of the Twelve, nor had he been among those who followed Him about during His life on earth, attracted by His wonderful works, and by the charm of His presence and of His words. He had marvellous revelations, it is true. Still he had "to learn Christ," as he himself expresses it, much in the same way as we have to do, by hearing about Him, by pondering what he heard, by remembering that all our Blessed Saviour had done and suffered was for him. "He loved me, and delivered Himself for me," was the thought that stirred all that was noble within him, and urged his generous nature to return love for love.

If we want to love our Lord fervently, to make Him some return for all His love to us, we must try to know Him by making ourselves familiar with His life. We must notice His ways—His gentleness and compassion; His tenderness with sinners, with the sick, the sorrowing, the little children; His faithfulness to His friends, His patience, His lovableness. We must try to bring home to ourselves, like St. Paul, that however poor and unimportant we may be in the eyes of others, however undeserving and sinful, we are each of us, one by one, clear and precious to the Heart of our Blessed Lord beyond what we are able to conceive. That for love of us one by one He taught, and toiled, and suffered. That had we been the only soul He came to save, He would have done for us singly what He has done for all. Each one of us, however lowly and unworthy, can say with the great Apostle: "He loved me, and delivered Himself for me." When we come to realise this in some degree, our hearts will begin to warm. We shall find that we have found what we all long to find—a true and faithful friend, a Friend who will never tire of us, who will put up with our shortcomings and our selfishness, and be always ready to listen to us and to help us. We shall begin to trust Him. We shall love to be with Him. We shall invite Him to come to us oftener, and prepare our hearts better to receive Him. And His visits will be more fruitful. Though the Sacraments work without our cooperation, their effects are stinted unless the soil is prepared. Our Lord could have worked a miracle in the desert to feed the hungry multitude without having bread to multiply. But His way is to help those who help themselves. He sent for the few little loaves that a boy in the crowd had brought, and blessed and multiplied them. So is it with our dispositions. He increases whatever good He finds.

And why should we not do all we can to make Him welcome for His own sake, as well as for what He brings us! He is our best of friends, with whom we are to spend our eternity; must we not be getting to know Him better, that we may love Him more? It was for us as well as for the sick of His own day that He showed Himself so tender and merciful. He knew we should one day hear of the kind things He said and did, and He wanted to draw our hearts to Himself by their means. We must ponder and try to make real to ourselves, now one, now another of His miracles of mercy; to enter into the feelings of thankfulness of those He healed, and to remember we have the very same tender Lord with us in Holy Communion, who wants us to treat with Him and to trust Him as if we had known and loved Him whilst He was here on earth.

I believe, O my Saviour; I believe firmly that Thou who art coming to visit me art the true Son of God who did come to Mary, lie in a manger, travel to and fro through the towns of Judea and by the seashore of Galilee. I believe Thou art the very same Lord who for me didst sweat blood beneath the olive trees and hang upon the cross. All this I believe. And yet I may cry with Saul on the way to Damascus: "Who art Thou, Lord?" Teach me more and more about Thyself. Bring home to me, make real to me what I hold by my faith. How is it I can believe so much yet love so little? Oh that I could love and trust Thee like those who knew Thee during Thy life on earth, whose hearts beat quickly at the thought of seeing Thy face, of hearing Thee calling them by their name!

But to love Thee devotedly it is not necessary to have seen Thee. "Because thou hast seen Me, Thomas, thou hast believed; blessed are those who have not seen, and have believed." Let this blessing be mine, dear Lord. Come to me, that I may know Thee better. Come to make Thyself more to my soul. Come and teach me how to speak to Thee, to unburden my heart to Thee, to trust to Thee its miseries, its weaknesses, its desire of better things.

I am sorry for all the sins which have dulled my mind to the divine truths I believe by faith. I am sorry for having often hardened my heart when I heard Thy voice speaking within me. Forgive me, O forgiving Lord, and come to me now to help me to a more fervent life in Thy service.

After Communion

Salvation to our God who sitteth upon the throne, the throne of His glory in heaven, the throne here on earth of my poor heart.

O ye Angels of the Lord, bless the Lord, praise and exalt Him above all for ever.

O ye servants of the Lord, bless the Lord, praise and exalt Him above all for ever.

Give praise to our God, all ye His servants, and you that fear Him, little and great.

O give thanks to the Lord because He is good, because His mercy endureth for ever.

Who art Thou, Lord? I know; I adore. Thou art Christ, the Son of the Living God. I bow myself down before Thee. I adore Thy sacred Body that suffered hunger and thirst, and cold, and weariness, and a cruel death for me. I adore Thy precious Blood that was poured out for me. I adore Thy Blessed Soul once sorrowful for me even unto death. I adore Thy Divinity by which Thou art one God with the Father and the Holy Ghost.

How can I thank Thee, my God, for giving me Thyself? Who will help me to bless and praise Thee? My soul doth magnify the Lord, and my spirit hath rejoiced in God my Saviour. For He that is mighty hath done great things to me, and holy is His name. With the thanksgiving of Thy Holy Mother, with the joyful praise of all Thy Angels and Saints, I thank, and bless, and praise Thee. O grant that I may praise Thee for ever.

Thou hast done great things for me, my God, and Thou hast come to do great things. Not till I get to Heaven and look back on my Communion days shall I understand all Thou hast done for me, silently, unknown even to myself, during these precious quarters of an hour of thanksgiving. Cold though I may be, and wandering in attention, Thy loving work for me goes on. The forgiveness of venial sin, the quieting of my passions, the weakening of bad habits, new joy in God's service, strength for future conflicts, growth in the love of Christ and in likeness to Christ—all good things come to me together with

Thee, dear Lord. What shall I render to the Lord for all He hath rendered unto me?

"My child, give Me thy heart. Give it to Me, for by the right of creation it is Mine. Give it to Me, for I have given the blood of My Heart to save it from misery and to purchase for it eternal joy. Give it to Me, who alone can make it happy. Give it to Me, that it may not be spoilt by self-seeking, by running too eagerly after the things of this life. Give it to Me, that it may not be disappointed in the end, that I may satisfy all its desires, all its craving for affection and for happiness, and be Myself its reward exceeding great."

Take, O Lord, and receive. I give Thee my heart. Who but Thyself would care for it! Who, knowing it as Thou dost, would not despise it! O God, who possessing the hearts of all Saints dost ask for mine, I offer it to Thee with humble thankfulness for the love that makes Thee ask it. Would it were an offering less unworthy of Thee. I give it to Thee that Thou mayst keep it safe, and that all its love may be Thine. And with it I give Thee all whom I love, to be kept in Thy service or to be brought back thereto. Guide us all through the perils of this short life, and make us worthy to possess and enjoy Thee forever in the life to come. Amen.

PETITION

"I will make him a pillar in the temple of my God."—Apoc. 3:12

I wish I could be a little pillar, my God, supporting something for Thee, no matter what; a pillar rough, unpolished, hidden away if Thou wilt, but doing a work for Thee.

In one way, at least, I may be a pillar. Thy interests all the world over are given into our keeping that we may uphold them all—by prayer.

Bring home to me, Lord, the responsibility that lies upon me to be earnest in prayer for all who are entrusted to me, or who are in any way brought within my influence. And not for these only, but for all my brethren, all my fellow-servants, every soul on the wide earth. They are Thy children, all of them, with a right to call Thee "Father," with their place in Thy Heart. Surely, then, they must have a place in mine.

I pray "for all that concerns the interests of Thy Kingdom on earth, for the Holy Father, for the diocese, for the Church in every land. For the foreign missions, for the temporal independence of the Pope, for persecuted religious abroad, for the safety of our schools in this country."

I pray that Thou mayst "reign in every heart, that the power of the Evil One may be broken and may come to naught, that Jesus Christ may everywhere conquer and triumph; that His law, His commandments, and His Church may rule the whole world; that there may be neither rebel, nor traitor, nor deserter, but that all may live under His rule, and in His grace, until they have to leave the earthly Kingdom for that which is prepared in Heaven."[1]

Prayer before a Crucifix, p. 12.

---

1   Bishop Hedley, Pastoral Letter, Lent, 1904.

THE WELCOME OF A FRIEND

II

"I will not now call you servants, but friends"—John 15:15.

Before Communion

FIRST among the privileges of perfect friendship, and comprising every other, is unreservedness of communication between us and our friend. Whatever befalls us he must know. We do not believe an event can be read aright unless his eye interprets it along with our own. The impression it makes upon us is largely determined by his judgment. Pain is softened, joy is doubled, by being shared with him. If it is an injustice or a disappointment that has upset us, we exaggerate the trouble of course, perhaps allow ourselves many an intemperate word that would be checked in any other presence. But he knows us so well; knows us in every mood; our way of looking at things; our infirmities of character; he will make allowances; it does not matter what we say to him. Everything may come out, and the outpouring will prevent effusions in quarters where they would be unjustifiable and unsafe.

Oh what a resource we have in human friendship! God Himself acknowledges and sanctions it when He tells us: "A steadfast friend shall be to Thee as thyself" (Ecclus. 6:11). "Open not thy heart to every man" (Ecclus. 8:22), "but let one of a thousand be thy counsellor" (Ecclus. 6:6). "A faithful friend is a strong defence, and he that hath found him hath found a treasure. Go to him early in the morning, and let thy foot wear the steps of his doors" (*Ibid.*).

Yet it does not suffice Him to give us friends frail and feeble as ourselves. Nor even to open to us the Courts of Heaven, and make us welcome to the friendship of those blessed ones whom He vouchsafes to own as friends. But He would Himself be our Friend. All the advantages of friendship heightened to an inconceivable degree; all the devotedness, faithfulness, resourcefulness, forbearance, which the annals of friendship or the wildest stretch of imagination can furnish, is but the feeblest image of what He offers—nay presses upon the acceptance of—every one of us.

"The soul of Jonathan was knit to the soul of David, and Jonathan loved him as his own soul" (1 Kings 18:1). But what was this union compared with that between us and our Blessed Lord in Holy Communion! We are engrafted in Him as the branch in the vine, a similitude of His own which should be pondered in detail till we come to realise something of its stupendous significance.

"And Jonathan stripped himself of the coat with which he was clothed and gave it to David, and the rest of his garments, even to his sword, and to his bow, and to his girdle." A paltry sacrifice indeed beside that of the Cross and of the Eucharist!

In the hour of need Jonathan interposed between his friend and his father's anger: "I will go and stand beside my father; I will speak of thee to my father. And Jonathan spoke good things of David to Saul, his father. And Saul was appeased by the words of Jonathan" (1 Kings 19:4,6). But "Christ loved us and delivered Himself for us" (Ephes. 5:2), "making peace with the blood of His cross" (Col. 1:20); "loved us and washed us from our sins in His own Blood" (Apoc. 1:5); "always living to make intercession for us" (Heb. 7:25).

The friendship between the prince and the shepherd fascinates us. Yet the love of the God of heaven and earth for such as we are fails to excite wonder or enthusiasm. All the beauty and pathos of human friendship is found in the Divine; sympathy, self-sinking, generosity, carried to a length impossible to surpass even in thought. But we take it all as a matter of course, and see no particular reason why the duty of gratitude should be so urged upon us.

And surely, O Lord, there should be none! Surely the sight of the Crucifix or the Tabernacle, the very thought of either, should melt our hearts and carry us out of ourselves with admiration and thankfulness. We extol the wide brotherhood of Francis of Assisi. We are charmed by his sympathy with the innocent things of the irrational creation. But his passionate love of Christ Crucified, the vehemence and the tenderness of his heart's outpouring the night through: "My God and my All!"—this we fail to understand, this wakes no echo in our own heart.

How long, O Lord, how long! Thou didst die for me as for Francis; draw my heart to Thee by a return of love. Make the Crucifix speak to my heart as to his. My God and my All, make Thyself more to my soul. There was a time when this seraph of the earth was wedded to earthly things. And Thy grace came and drew his whole affection to Thee, and now he is associated in our minds with the burning spirits before Thy throne. Give Thy grace to me too, mean and miserable as I am. Canst Thou refuse Thy grace who dost give Thyself? I long to love Thee, my God, with a love less unworthy of Thee. Help me to love Thee. Take from my heart all obstacles to Thy love. Let me love Thee with my whole heart, with my whole soul, with all my mind, with all my strength before I come to die, that I may love Thee according to Thy desire throughout eternity.

AFTER COMMUNION

"Blessed be the Lord for this day" (3 Kings 5:7).

"Blessed be the Lord, for He hath shown His wonderful mercy to me" (Ps. 30:22).

"For He hath satisfied the empty soul, and hath filled the hungry soul with good things" (Ps. 106:9).

"O my soul, bless the Lord, and let all that is within me bless His holy Name" (Ps. 102:1).

"Bless the Lord, O my soul, and never forget all He hath done for thee" (*Ibid.*).

"Give glory to the Lord for He is good, for His mercy endureth for ever" (Ps. 106:1).

"What shall I render to the Lord for all that He hath rendered to me?" (Ps. 115:12).

"I will extol Thee, O God my King, and I will bless Thy name for ever, yea for ever and ever" (Ps. 144:1).

"O my soul, bless thou the Lord" (Ps. 103:35).

"And when they had adored God and given Him thanks, they sat down together" (Tobias 11:12).

Here is the right ordering of our thanksgiving after Communion—God's claims first, and, these satisfied, the familiar intercourse with our Lord and the setting forth of our needs. Though, indeed, the satisfying of God's claims is the first and deepest of our needs.

How is it to be brought about? His due is nothing short of the infinite, and our very best is finite. Oh how miserably finite we feel when we come to deal with God! But—thanks be to God for His unspeakable Gift—what is absolutely impossible for us to do, is perfectly done for us by the Incarnation, and by the extension of the Incarnation: the Eucharist.

Our Lord places Himself upon the altar, within easy reach of every one of us. He puts His Sacred Heart at our disposal, bidding us help ourselves freely from its treasures, and pay thus to the last farthing the debt we owe. To provide us with an adoration, praise, and thanksgiving worthy of Himself, is His chief motive in remaining with us all days; in offering Himself on the altar every day; in coming to us in

Holy Communion whenever we will. By Him, with Him, in Him, we, little finite creatures, nothing of ourselves, worse than nothing by our sinfulness, can give to the supreme God a worship that He accepts as sufficient, by which every Perfection receives its full meed of adoration and praise, good measure, pressed down, shaken together, running over.

"He that is mighty hath done great things for me," we may cry out in our joy, as we look at the Tabernacle, and fold our hands over our breast after Communion. He has perfected praise even in the mouth of such a one as I. For I am not alone; Jesus is with me. "I will rejoice in the Lord, and I will joy in God my Jesus" (Habacuc 3:18).

"And when they had adored God, and given Him thanks, they sat down together."

He wants now to hear about ourselves—how things are going with us—how we have been getting on since He was with us last. Is union with Him strengthening? Does the sap flow more freely, more continuously from the Vine into the branch? Are we getting, little by little, to live by Him? Is there communion of tastes, interests, joys, and sorrows? Interchange of loving offices? Is there devotedness to His cause at the cost of personal sacrifice? Does all that touches Him affect us more than it did once? Is He coming to be, almost unconsciously to ourselves, the main need of our life?

And what about our work for Him—about the anxiety common to us both for those we love, those whose names He sees upon our lips whenever we come to Him? And other things. The interview we talked over with Him—how did it go off? The cloud in that other quarter—is it lifting? He wants to know all. Have we come to Him that He may share our gladness? Or is it the old sympathy, the sympathy of years on which we must draw still? Oh that fellow-feeling of His Sacred Human Heart, not only ready ever, but fresh as ever—a constancy impossible in other friends! They must tire. They do tire. They brace themselves up to give us a patient hearing once again. They try—what more can they do?—to draw upon the resources of their faithful hearts. But they are sensible, almost as much as we are, how feebly, almost mechanically, the words of sympathy come, not from fault of theirs, but simply because the strain has been so long.

> "Oh when the heart is full, when bitter thoughts
>   Come crowding thickly up for utterance,
>   And the poor common words of courtesy
>   Are such a very mockery—how much
>   The bursting heart may pour itself in prayer!"[1]

---

1 Willis

"Come to Me when it is not well with thee" (*Imit.*). His invitation is as pressing the hundredth and the thousandth time as it was at first. "Come to Me you who are heavy-laden, and I will refresh you." His Heart does not sink when He sees us coming. Nay, His delight is to see us take up our post before the Tabernacle: too weary, perhaps, to pray—but just to sit before Him, our eyes upon the little door, waiting for our refreshment. The sympathy of the Heart beating there is infinite. It never fails, nor can fail. When the need ceases, when the long waiting is rewarded, and the time has come for Him to share our joy as He has shared our pain—then, and not till then, will there be change in the patient Listener there.

Oblation and Petition, p. 82.

Prayer before a Crucifix, p. 12.

THE WELCOME OF A FRIEND

III

Moods.

BEFORE COMMUNION

AMONG the treasures of friendship on which we have to draw most largely and continuously, is forbearance. It is not so much that our wants are many and importunate, as that our moods are so shifting. Our phases, like the moon's, are regular at least in their inconstancy. They come and go, affecting the brightness of life within and without, and we can no more prevent these alternations than the queen of night can keep herself always at the full. "Sometimes joyful, at other times sad; now easy, anon troubled; at one time devout, at another dry; sometimes fervent, at other times sluggish; one day heavy, another lighter," says one who knew human nature well. And he has but given a sample of our fluctuations. Capricious, irresolute, fastidious, fretful, sulky, restive, stubborn, we are a riddle to all, save to Him who made us. What should we do without a divine friendship to fall back upon! Our Lord is our resource in every mood. He adapts Himself to each with a readiness and a grace that imply no reproach. His invitation never tires: "Come to Me, and I will refresh you." We are always welcome. There is no sign that our waywardness or our perversity jars upon Him. He receives us with a graciousness that soothes while it shames us. He hears out our one-sided tale without expostulation or rebuke. And when the consciousness of His tender interest has drawn our trouble from us, and the outlet of our heart into His has relieved and quieted us, He comes with His gentle touch and heals our wounds, pouring in oil and wine, and sends us again on our way with lightened and braver hearts.

"Go thou and do likewise," is His word to us. For His friendship is not our resource only, but our exemplar. O Lord, how little have I sought to mould myself as a friend on Thee! In my relations with those around me, the leading characteristics of friendship have place always. The exercise of authority may be called for at one time, of submission at another, but the self-abnegation, the forbearance, the resourcefulness of a friend are needed at all times and with all. Jesus, Divine Friend, make my heart like unto Thine.

In His dealings with others how striking is the self-forgetfulness, the divine charity with which our Lord lays Himself out to meet the need of the moment. Is it to draw our attention to this that St. Matthew recounts for us the calls upon His attention and sympathy in a single day?

He was teaching where "many had come together, so that there was no room, no not even at the door."

"And behold they brought to Him one sick of the palsy lying in a bed. And Jesus said to the man sick of the palsy, … Arise, take up thy bed, and go into thy house.…

"And when Jesus passed on from thence, He saw a man sitting in the custom-house, named Matthew; and He saith to him: Follow Me.

"Then came to Him the disciples of John, saying: Why do we and the Pharisees fast often, but Thy disciples do not fast?…

"And as He was speaking to them, behold a certain ruler came up and adored Him, saying: Lord, my daughter is even now dead; but come, lay Thy hand upon her, and she shall live. And Jesus rising up followed him, with His disciples" (Matt. 9:18).

And having on the way thither healed the woman who touched the hem of His garment for her cure, He came to where Jairus' little daughter lay dead. "And He took her by the hand, and the maid arose" (*Ibid.*) "And He commanded that something should be given her to eat" (Mark 5:43).

"And as He passed from thence, there followed Him two blind men crying out and saying, Have mercy on us, O Son of David. . . . And He touched their eyes and their eyes were opened. . . .

"And when they were gone out, behold they brought Him a dumb man, possessed with a devil. And when the devil was cast out, the dumb man spoke" (Matt. 9:32).

This is a sample of one of His days.

It was not only the laying of His hands on these afflicted ones that drew the multitudes after Him, "so that they trod one upon another," it was the words of sympathy that accompanied His healing touch. "Be of good heart, son, thy sins are forgiven thee." "Fear not, only believe." "Be of good heart, daughter, go in peace, and be thou whole of thy disease." "*Talitha, cumi*," "Maiden, arise."

In the expression of His face, in the tones of His voice, there was no trace of a hard day's teaching as He took the little children into His arms. As He "embraced them, and laid His hands upon them, and blessed them," no cloud upon His brow told of the bitter disappointment at hand when the young man whom He loved would turn away sorrowful from His invitation.   The burden of sin and sorrow that continually pressed upon Him did not engross Him or prevent Him from entering with the most tender solicitude into the sorrows of others. His Heart was wrung with anguish as He sat gazing for the last time on His dear Jerusalem, so soon to be beaten flat to the ground and her children within her. Yet He noted with admiration and compassion the mite that dropped into the corbona, the widow's offering of all she had.

None feared to approach Him; He was at every one's beck and call. The guileless Nathaniel, the notorious Magdalen, the earnest seeker after truth, the thoughtless, the selfish, the caviller, all met with the same courteous kindness. All found Him leisured, considerate, gentle, helpful. There was no mistaking the fellow-feeling revealed by His glance, His smile, the words that fell from His lips. There was no mistrusting His welcome. Each sufferer that knelt at His feet was conscious of being just the one He most wanted to see, the one for whom He was waiting. Who would have guessed that He knew those long tales better than the tellers; that this Friend of publicans and sinners was the God who abhors iniquity; that He to whose lips praise came so readily was the All-perfect, the searcher of hearts? He was not exacting. He welcomed good wherever He found it, a little where He could discern no more. The bruised reed He did not break, and smoking flax He did not extinguish. His sympathy never failed or flagged. If, as night fell, His face betrayed signs of weariness, not so His ear or His Heart. The last suppliant found Him as attractive, as attentive as the first that had disturbed His prayer at break of day.

And thus I find Him after all His experience of me—patient, tender, devoted, bearing all things, hoping all things, making Himself all things to me that He may win me to Himself, win me to a greater likeness to Him in mind and heart.

"Shouldst not thou have compassion on thy fellow-servant even as I have compassion on thee? I have given you an example that as I have done to you, so you do also."

O Jesus, Divine Friend, my resource in the ever-varying moods and needs of life, have patience with me and help me. Come to me today to work a change in my heart. Let me learn of Thee. Let me imitate Thee. Warm the coldness of my selfish nature. Soften my hardness. Fill me with the burning, self-sacrificing charity of Thy divine Heart. Make my heart like unto Thine.

After Communion

"This is the Christ" (Acts 9:22).

"This is God, our God unto eternity, and for ever and ever" (Ps. 47:15).

"Whence is this to me that my Lord should come to me?"

"*Adoro te devote, latens Deitas.*"

Devoutly I adore Thee, O hidden Deity.

"Verily Thou art a hidden God" (Isa. 45:15).

"O love the Lord, all ye His saints" (Ps. 30:24).

"Give glory to the Lord for He is good, for His mercy endureth for ever" (Ps. 105:1).

"Come, let us praise the Lord with joy, let us joyfully sing to God our Saviour" (Ps. 94:1).

"Let the mercies of the Lord give glory to Him, and His wonderful works to the children of men" (Ps. 106:8).

Love shows itself by a communication of gifts. What does our Lord give me this morning? A Gift than which He has nothing greater or better to bestow. A Gift that cannot be merited; that has no equivalent;

that comprises all that is; that is infinite in dignity and in worth—the Body and Blood, Soul and Divinity of God made Man.

And this infinite Gift is enhanced by the way in which it is bestowed. He gives Himself as a pledge of His love, a pledge of eternal life, a pledge we may have daily if we will. Nay, more, as a fountain of living water, springing up even now and here into life everlasting. All that is needed for purifying, enlightening, strengthening, satisfying my soul, for ensuring my eternal salvation, and that finished likeness to Christ in which perfection consists, is given to me here. O truly Blessed Sacrament, how hath He not with thee given us all things!

And what do I give Him in return? Lord, it is not much, but it is all I have. I give Thee myself, body and soul. I give Thee my life, strength, desires, resolutions, efforts, all my love and my trust, my joys and my anxieties, my aspirations after better things, my labour for the souls that Thou lovest.

Freely I have received, freely let me give. Let the sense of my own infirmity, my own need of sympathy and encouragement, make me alive to the need of others. My own moods come and go. I find myself hard to handle. I am a trial to those about me. May I be tender and compassionate to those who, like myself, are struggling with nature and are occasionally worsted in the fight. Let me accommodate myself to them at times when they need indulgence; overlook what is unreasonable and trying; pass unnoticed what is the outcome of worry, or disappointment, or fatigue.

Teach me, dear Lord, how to lighten the burdens of others; how, without gossiping, to listen to and feel with those in trouble, not inflicting useless advice, not wearying with barren sympathy, but exerting myself to be really helpful. Show me how to deal prudently and tactfully with difficulties, taking heed lest, instead of drawing out a sting, I envenom it.

I ask of Thee, Lord, the spirit of gentleness; a compassionate heart fashioned after the likeness of Thine own; tender to the sick, the weak, the erring, the little children, the mourners; eager to pursue at the cost of labour and weariness, at the risk of rebuff, even one soul; ready to give generously time, interest, sympathy, self-denying help to those in need.

Let the sight of Thee halting on the road to Calvary to speak to the women of Jerusalem—forgetting the throbbing, thorn-crowned head, the lacerated body, the agonising soul, to think of them, to provide for them—have force to take me out of myself in pain of body and mind; to make me forget my own grievances in order to bring to others sympathy and help.

I ponder the first words from the Cross; the strong cry for Thy crucifiers; the merciful promise to the robber by Thy side; the filial provision for Thy disconsolate Mother. But I forget the intolerable anguish of body and of soul in which those words were spoken. It was the most awful of death throes, the fiercest pangs of dereliction that were calmly put aside to make way for the needs of others. Ah, Lord, and a slight headache or annoyance, a little press of work, is enough to make me preoccupied, inconsiderate and churlish to all around me!

Dear Master, have patience with me. Teach me the lesson of sacrifice Thou hast taught to so many. Let me learn it from my crucifix. Let me learn it from the daily Sacrifice of Thyself upon our altars. Let me learn it from the Host within my breast, Love's supreme effort to humble itself to us, to spend itself for us, to prove its delights are to be with the dear children of men.

Oblation and Petition, p. 82.

Prayer before a Crucifix, p. 12.

THE WELCOME OF A
PATIENT

THE WELCOME OF A PATIENT

I

"Virtue went out from Him and healed all"—Luke 6:19.

"And whithersoever He entered, into towns or into villages, they laid the sick in the streets, and besought Him that they might touch but the hem of His garment; and as many as touched Him were made whole"—Mark 6:56.

Before Communion

WHAT excitement there must have been when He was expected in a town; what eagerness of the sick; what joy of their friends as they laid them in rows along the narrow streets to await His coming! Here a group of children round a dying father. Here a mother, bedridden for years, propped up by her daughters. Here, at a corner, a little boy with his blind grandfather. All watching, waiting, with breathless impatience.

All, not hoping, but knowing their sick will go home cured—the father in the midst of his rejoicing family; the mother walking between her daughters; the blind man of so many years looking with delight on the face of his little grandson and guide. Can we realise such a state of things, such expectancy, such jubilation? The extra place at table prepared at home before they set out: the sick-room for which there will be no further need, tidied up: the children keeping watch on the road to catch the first sight of our Lord: their shouts of joy when along the white dusty way appear signs of His crowd!

And He is coming today—to me!

Thy visit will remind Thee, O Lord, of the old days in Galilee and Judea when there pressed round Thee a crowd of deaf and dumb, palsied, and lame, and blind. And I shall be reminded of those blessed days when Thou, laying Thy hand on every one of them, healed them. Thy work in my soul is more directly that which brought Thee down from heaven, than the cure of bodily disease. If Thou wert pleased to show Thyself so liberal in the lesser need, it was to encourage me to draw near to Thee, to touch Thee in Holy Communion with faith and hope, to lay open to Thee, divine Physician, the wounds of my soul that

Thou mayst heal them. This is what I have come to do now. Look on me kneeling at Thy feet, and pity me and help me.

I am leprous—covered with the unsightly and dangerous sores of my many sins. Lord, if Thou wilt, Thou canst make me clean. Say to me: "I will; be thou made clean."

I am sick and weak—forever halting on the upward road; soon tired; easily discouraged; unequal to serious or prolonged effort; always looking out for ease and rest.

I am blind. What others see clearly is dim and confused to me. That eternity is coming, and coming fast; that I must prepare for death and judgment; that I can only live my life once—all this I believe as the blind man believes in colour. But such belief is not enough for me to square my life by. The eyes of my soul must be opened to perceive what I hold by faith. Lord, that I may see!

I am blind to the beauties of material creation that mirror Thee, the Eternal, Uncreated Beauty, and that lose their meaning unless they lift my soul to Thee in thanksgiving and praise. I am blind to the far fairer creations of grace in the souls of those around me. So little serves to obscure my sight. So thin a veil hides Thee from me. How often a keener faith, a truer appreciation would descry, shining through the human frailty that scandalises me, the beauty of the spirit made to Thy likeness, my God! Lord, that I may see, that I may see!

I am blind to my faults, prompt, at least, to excuse in myself what I heartily condemn in another. I am negligent in my duty of supervision, blind to harm going on around me which I ought to know and check and for which I shall be held accountable. My God, illuminate my darkness. Lord, that I may see!

I am deaf. Inspirations come and I heed them not. I know they are Thy voice, prompting or reproaching me, suggesting a good thought, a kind word or act. But if obedience to them involves trouble or self-sacrifice, I pretend not to hear. Make me more honest, more generous with Thee, my God. Let me be glad to know Thy Will in great things, in little things, in things that cost. Let it be a real prayer when I say: "Speak, Lord, for Thy servant heareth."

I am dumb. Not in the company of those needy like myself, unwilling to aid, or powerless. But in Thine, O my Father, who art rich in mercy, who givest to all abundantly, and with loving insistence dost press upon me Thy good gifts. In the presence of Thy Beauty and Thy Goodness I am mute. No praise wells up in my heart; no cry for mercy comes to my lips. I have no eager welcome for Thee who dost come so far to be my Guest. O Lord, open Thou my lips, and my mouth shall declare Thy praise. Set my heart free to pour itself out before Thee. Teach me to pray, that by prayer I may obtain from Thee the supply of all I need.

Leprous, palsied, blind, deaf, dumb—surely I need the visit of the Physician!

"Take courage and fear not. Behold your God Himself will come and will save you. Then shall the eyes of the blind be opened, and the ears of the deaf shall be unstopped. Then shall the lame man leap as a hart, and the tongue of the dumb shall be free" (Isa.35:4).

"Our soul waiteth for the Lord, for He is our Helper and Protector" (Ps. 32:20).

"The eyes of all hope in Thee, O Lord. . . . Thou openest Thy hand and fillest with blessing every living creature" (Ps. 144:15).

Jesus, Son of David, have mercy on me. Son of David, have mercy on me.

AFTER COMMUNION

"I adore the Lord my God, for He is the living God" (Dan. 14:24).

"Adore Him, all you His Angels" (Ps. 96:7).

"Exalt ye the Lord our God" (Ps. 98:5).

"O magnify the Lord with me, and let us extol His Name together" (Ps. 33:4).

"I will give glory to the Lord, and will sing to the Name of the Lord the Most High" (Ps. 7:18).

"I will praise Thee, O Lord my God, with my whole heart, and I will glorify Thy Name for ever" (Ps. 85:12).

"Bless the Lord, O my soul, and let all that is within me bless His Holy Name" (Ps. 102:1).

"Who forgiveth all thy iniquities, who healeth all thy diseases" (*Ibid.*).

"Blessed be the Name of His Majesty for ever. So be it. So be it" (Ps. 71:19).

"The Lord will take away from thee all sickness and the grievous infirmities which thou knowest" (Deut. 7:15).

"More friendly than a brother" (Prov. 18:24), dearest Lord, Thou didst show Thyself to all the sorrowing and heavy-laden. No sores were too loathsome for Thy touch; no sickness however inveterate but had to yield to Thy word: "All they that had any disease were brought to Him, and He, laying His hand on every one of them, healed them."

And Thou—the same as then—art with me now. With the same—nay, with greater compassion, Thou dost behold the wounds of my soul. I am too apt to think that while the infirmities of the body call for Thy pity, Thou hast only anger and indignation for those of the soul. Yet Thy gentleness with sinners and Thy tender handling of their wounds should teach me confidence. I cast myself, then, at Thy feet. I place myself beneath Thy healing hand. I wait for the word that will cure, though not all at once, my pride, my hastiness of temper, my coldness in prayer, my uncharitable tongue, my neglect of distasteful duties. Lord, if Thou wilt, Thou canst. Say but the word!

The doctor, when he comes on his rounds, expects from the ward Sister an intelligent account of her patient's condition. She should show an accurate chart of pulse, respiration, temperature. She must be able to report on sleep or the want of it, and on any change in the nature or in the chief features of the disease. She is eyes and ears to the doctor in his absence, and his treatment depends to a great extent on her watchfulness and truthful statement of what she sees and hears.

I am the nurse appointed to tend my sick soul. And I am ashamed to own that I am a very indifferent, not to say careless nurse. I shirk work. I take little trouble to ascertain the wants of my charge. I expose it to injury. I neglect its food and medicine. I sleep when I should watch. What account can I give when my knowledge is so superficial and all my nurse's instincts are at fault?

Happily the Divine Physician knows all. He needs not that any should give testimony of man, for He knows what is in man. "For every heart is understood by Him" (Ecclus. 16:20). "The eyes of the Lord behold the good and the evil" (Prov. 15:3). "All the ways of a man are open to His eyes" (*Ibid.*).

All-wise and compassionate Physician, forgive my negligence. To Thee I commit my charge. "O God, I beseech Thee, heal her" (Num. 12:13). Have pity on her because she is my only one. And give me the instincts and the virtues of my calling, in which I am so sadly wanting. Nursing demands untiring energy, vigilance, cheerfulness, and an inexhaustible stock of patience. There is the trouble necessary for ascertaining the nature of the disease—its supposed cause, its time and mode of onset—with a view to its proper treatment. There is the marking of the chart morning and evening. There is watching day and night. There is firmness to withhold unwise indulgence. There is medicine and feeding timed. Then the mending is so slow. Temperature rises at the least provocation. The patient will do what is imprudent, and there are relapses, and all the treatment has to be begun over again. Monotonous work when it goes on year after year. More monotonous, perhaps, when the patient to be treated is my own soul.

Never to weary of the daily round of duty, of the vigilance, the precautions, the relapses; never to despair of my charge—Lord, it is hard. What should we do, "I and my soul" (Tobias 13:9), but for the cheering visits of the Physician? He is long-suffering and kind. He is prepared for anything in the shape of capriciousness, restlessness, perversity. He shows neither surprise, nor disgust, nor disappointment; bearing all things, believing all things, hoping all things. Today with bright eager faces we welcome Him to our bedside. Tomorrow, heavy and discouraged, we have scarcely a word of thanks for His coming. He takes us as we are. He knows our imperfect being. We have not to deal with one who cannot have compassion on our infirmities, but with Him who has said: "They that are whole need not the physician, but they that are sick" (Luke 5:31).

Courage, then, my soul! "Is not He thy Father that hath possessed thee, and made thee, and created thee?"

(Deut. 32:6). "A forgiving God, gracious and merciful, long-suffering and full of compassion" (2 Esdras 9:17). "He is mighty to forgive" (Ecclus. 16:12). "He will have mercy on thee more than a mother" (Ecclus. 4:11). "The Lord will take away from thee all sickness and the grievous infirmities which thou knowest. He raiseth up the soul, and enlighteneth the eyes, and giveth health, and life, and blessing" (Ecclus. 34:20). "This only take care of with all diligence, that you love the Lord your God" (Jos. 23:11).

"I will close up thy scar, and will heal thee of thy wounds, saith the Lord" (Jer. 30:17).

"Heal me, O Lord, and I shall be healed; save me, and I shall be saved" (Jer. 17:14).

Oblation and Petition, p. 10.

Prayer before a Crucifix, p. 12.

THE WELCOME OF A PATIENT

II

"He, laying His hands on every one of them,
healed them"—Luke 4:40.

BEFORE COMMUNION

TWO things strike us specially in the account of our Lord's cures—their number, and their being due in almost every case to contact with the Sacred Humanity. "And coming to her He lifted her up, taking her by the hand" (Mark 1:31). "And Jesus stretched forth His hand, and touching him saith to him: I will, be thou made clean" (*Ibid.*). "Then He touched their eyes...and their eyes were opened" (Matt. 9:29). "He put His fingers into his ears, and touched his tongue. And immediately his ears were opened and the string of his tongue was loosed" (Mark 7:33-35). That life and healing lay in His simple touch was well known: "Come, lay Thy hand upon her and she shall live" (Matt. 9:18). "They brought to Him a blind man, and they besought Him that He would touch Him" (Mark 8:22). "If I shall touch but His garment I shall be whole" (Mark 5:28). "All the multitude sought to touch Him, for virtue went out from Him and healed all" (Luke 6:19).

Note the repetition of the word "all" in reference to our Lord's cures. "Jesus went about all Galilee… healing all manner of sickness and every infirmity among the people. And His fame went throughout all Syria, and they presented to Him all sick people that were taken with divers diseases and torments, and such as were possessed by devils, and lunatics, and those that had the palsy, and He cured them" (Matt. 4:23-24). And when the sun was down, all they that had any sick with divers diseases, brought them to Him. But He laying His hands on every one of them, healed them (Luke 4:40).

In no case, indeed, are we told of His touching any sufferer actually possessed by the devil. He "commanded" or "threatened" the evil spirit and he went out. But as soon as the poor victim was freed from his thraldom, he was permitted close approach to his Saviour. "They found the man out of whom the devils were departed, sitting at His feet" (Luke 8:35). "And crying out and greatly tearing him, the devil went out of him, and he became as one dead....But Jesus taking Him by the hand lifted him up" (Mark 9:25-26).

The same law holds good now. The soul that has actually given itself over to "the most wicked one" by mortal sin may not dare in that state to draw near by Sacramental Communion to "the Holy One of God." But the instant that by a good confession it is restored to grace, it may enjoy His intimate Presence by whom it has been healed.

It is characteristic of the Son of Man to will that cure should come from contact with His sacred flesh. During His life on earth it was the exception when He healed at a distance. But healing was dealt out broadcast to those who put themselves within reach of His touch. "He, laying His hands on every one of them, healed them." Not a word about merits. They came to Him. That was enough. He healed them.

"Behold the hand of the Lord is not shortened" (Isa. 59:1). He wills that virtue should go out from Him still. His complaint is still: "You will not come to Me that you may have life" (John 5:40). His promise holds good from age to age: "He that eateth Me, the same also shall live by Me. He that eateth My flesh and drinketh My blood hath everlasting life, and I will raise him up at the last day" (John 6:55). And His threat, too, holds good: "Except you eat the flesh of the Son of Man and drink His blood, you shall not have life in you" (*Ibid.*).

True, certain conditions are required. We must "prove ourselves," as the Apostle says. We must not give Him the kiss of Judas, and draw near to Him in order to betray Him. Is this asking too much? It is all He asks. At least it is all He strictly requires. The man who last night was in mortal sin, His enemy, meriting eternal banishment from Him, may, restored to grace this morning, draw near to embrace Him, to receive from Him the kiss of peace and the welcome due to a friend. It helps us to know how little He exacts. Not that we shall content ourselves with that little, but that, set at rest as to the fulfillment of His easy conditions, we may approach Him, as He so earnestly desires, with the love that casteth out fear.

Lord, I am not worthy that Thou shouldst enter under my roof. I am not worthy—but I have a right. The starving poor may take food where and how they can; their right is their need. The sick poor may come to the dispensary and have their ailments cared for "without money and without any price." Thus it is that I claim Thee, O Bread of Life, O remedy of all my ills. Thou knowest my soul through and through, its weakness, its dangerous diseases, its need of Thy healing touch. And never was remedy so near. Not His garment, but Himself, Body and Blood, and Soul, and Divinity given as medicine to my soul. Again, as in the days of His life on earth, He goes to and fro amongst us, healing all manner of sickness and every infirmity. Again there come to Him the blind and the lame in the Temple, "pressing upon Him for to touch Him, as many as have evils" (Mark 3:1).

"O kind Physician, I come to Thee; I commit myself to Thy hands. Heal me, O Lord, and I shall be healed; save me, and I shall be saved" (Jer. 17:14). Give me that Good in which is all good, which is life, vigour, growth, the cure of every disease, the satisfying of every need. For how hast Thou not with Thyself given us all things!

After Communion

Adoro Te, devote, latens Deitas.
Devoutly I adore Thee, O Hidden God,
"Adore Him, all you His Angels" (Ps. 96:7).
"Exalt ye the Lord our God" (Ps. 98:5).
"O magnify the Lord with me, and let us extol His Name together" (Ps. 33:4).
"Because He that is mighty hath done great things to me, and holy is His Name" (Luke 1:49).

"Bless the Lord, O my soul, and let all that is within me bless His holy Name" (Ps. 102:1).

"Bless the Lord, O my soul, and never forget all He hath done for thee" (Ps. 102:2).

"Who forgiveth all thy iniquities, who healeth all thy diseases" (*Ibid.*).

"He raiseth up the soul and enlighteneth the eyes, and giveth health, and life, and blessing" (Ecclus. 34:20).

"Heal me, O Lord, and I shall be healed; save me, and I shall be saved" (Jer. 17:14).

"Heal my soul, for I have sinned against Thee" (Ps. 40:5).

"O God, I beseech Thee, heal her" (Num. 12:13).

I adore Thee profoundly, O Sacred Humanity of my Saviour, source of all our good:

O face on which the angels desire to look, on which Mary looked continually, and worshipped with the adoration of the creature and the delight of the Mother's heart—I adore Thee.

O hands that lay swathed in the manger and fastened with cruel nails to the Cross: that cured every disease and every infirmity; that cooled the wasting heat of the fever-stricken, and were laid so tenderly on our sores; that gave sight to the blind, and hearing to the deaf, and strength and grace to the palsied and the deformed—I adore you here truly present, and commit myself to you for healing and for blessing!

O feet that went wearily to and fro seeking the lost sheep; that were anointed and kissed by Magdalen and held fast for the adoration of the faithful women on the morning of their resurrection from the dead—I adore you and bless you, and kiss the dear wounds you bore for me!

O Heart which had compassion on the hungry and the shepherdless, on the widow and the outcast, and poor perverse Jerusalem; that beat quicker at the welcome of those who loved Thee, and wert sorrowful even unto death at the desertion and betrayal of Thine own; O Heart that loved me and delivered Thyself for me, that art beating now with love for me close to my own poor heart—I adore Thee and bless Thee for all Thou hast done and suffered for my salvation, for all the wonders Thou hast wrought to give Thyself to me today!

Let me see, my God, by Thy divine light, the hidden things of my own heart, those things that my pride keeps from me. As long as I turn away my eyes from what is repulsive in me, I shall be in darkness; there will be a veil between myself and Thee. "Rabboni, that I may see!" The cry of the blind man of Jericho is my cry. Let me know myself and know Thee; know myself that I may come to know Thee. If Thou art not to me what Thou art to Thy Saints, it is because I do not know Thee as they do. I do not see as they see Thy Beauty, Thy Goodness, Thy Tenderness, Thy Love. Lord, that I may see!—see Thy beauty in all the mysteries of Thy blessed life; Thy goodness in all Thou hast done for me; Thy tenderness in Thy Real Presence with me, and in the forgiveness of my many sins; Thy love in all that happens to me. Lord, make me quick to see Thee everywhere and in all things— Lord, that I may see!

My God, I believe. I am cold, hard, dry, but I believe firmly in Thy Real Presence within me. I believe that Thou art nearer to me than to the friends of Thy life on earth, who received Thee under their roofs, who were rocked with Thee in Peter's boat, who led Thee to their sick and to the grave of their dead, who brought their little children to Thy feet.

My God, I hope in Thee. Not as I ought when I think of Thy mercies to me, and of Thy promises. But I trust Thee and trust myself to Thee, with all I have, with all I love, all my interests, all I need for my happiness in this life and the next. Give me light to see Thy goodness in all things that I may trust Thee more. Let me count on Thee like Martha and Mary, and cast all my care on Thee, certain that every prayer is heard, that Thou wilt bring help in Thy own time and in the best time.

My God, I love Thee. Not as Thy goodness deserves to be loved, but as much as I can love Thee now. Enkindle my heart with the love of Thy own now so near to mine.

My God, I long to sorrow for my sins purely for Thy sake, for love of Thee. Wert Thou to offer me one of two graces: perfect contrition or final perseverance, I think I should choose the first. Yet I must have that last grace that will put me in possession of Thee for ever. Then give them both to me that for all eternity I may glorify the mercy that has been so good, so good to me, a sinner.

Oblation & Petition, pp. 160, 162.

Prayer before a Crucifix, p. 12.

THE WELCOME OF A PATIENT

III

"Is there no physician there? Why, then, is not the wound of the daughter of My people closed?" —Jer. 8:22.

WHY? Perhaps through some want of docility to the prescriptions of the Physician; through some imprudence in venturing rashly into occasions of harm. Perhaps because He sees fit to work a gradual cure. It is not with sick souls as with the generality of the infirm of Judea and Galilee in the days of His Ministry. The healing of these was instantaneous. But this is not His usual way of dealing with spiritual ailments. Their cure, like that of the blind man of Bethsaida, is worked by little and little. "And laying His hands on him He asked him if he saw anything. And looking up, he said: I see men as it were trees walking. After that again He laid His hands upon his eyes and he began to see, and was restored, so that he saw all things clearly" (Mark 8:23).

If I want a perfect restoration I must bring myself often within His reach. I must feel again and again the touch of the Divine hands. It needs no great penetration into the counsels of God to see the gain to me of this His usual way of leading souls to sanctification. Left for a time, perhaps for a very long time, to struggle with my evil inclinations, I learn humility and patience, and find continual occasions of merit. Meantime, amid alternate manifestations of strength and weakness, the work goes forward, especially in the precious moments when the great Physician is with me, by His Presence and His touch perfecting my cure.

How little improvement the three years' close companionship with our Lord seemed to work in the Twelve. They noticed no striking change in one another; they were conscious of none in themselves. But He saw a steady transformation going forward, and rejoiced. He saw how the love of Himself, which brings with it all good, was gradually raising their standards, was widening, purifying, and kindling their hearts, and preparing the material for the fire which at Pentecost was to descend upon them and transform

them into other men. Slowly and quietly, as is the wont
with the works of God, they grew in the knowledge
and likeness of the Son of God, till each in his measure
and capacity, and according to the designs of God over
him, became *alter Christus*, a second Christ. So will it
be with us. Those about us—nay, we ourselves—may
see no appreciable difference in our lives for many a
day. Our many imperfections, our clinging selfishness,
may seem to clog our way as persistently as ever. But
we must not lose heart. "And he put his mouth
upon his mouth, and his eyes upon his eyes, and his
hands upon his hands . . . and the child's flesh grew
warm" (4 Kings 4:34). To a closer union still our Lord
condescends that He may warm my frozen heart. Not
all at once, but surely, His Heart close to mine will
kindle it. I shall know it. I shall feel it. I shall be
constrained to say with humble gratitude to the God
of the Eucharist: "He that is mighty hath done great
things for me."

I must bear in mind, however, that dispositions
count for much in this transformation. Though the
Holy Eucharist by the mere fact of its reception in a
state of grace adds to the soul's merit here and glory
hereafter, yet, like the seed sown in varying degrees
of good soil, its fruit will be here thirty, here sixty,
here a hundredfold. In one Communion is grace

enough to cure every disease and supply every need. But our imperfect dispositions hinder the effect of the Sacrament and interfere sadly with the loving designs of our Lord, who comes to us eager to enrich and make us happy.

Oh, that He would satisfy this desire of His, and for His own sake would prepare His way and increase the capacity of our souls! "Open thy mouth wide and I will fill it" (Ps. 80:11), He says. "You that thirst, come to the waters" (Isa. 55:1).

My God, there is so much to be done in my soul. So much to be purified, enlightened, warmed, remodelled, restored. So much lost time to be repaired; so much grace forfeited to be made good; so many missed opportunities that, alas, can never return, to be compensated by more strenuous efforts now. O Lord, help me, make haste to help me. Remember that all power is given Thee in heaven and on earth. "Thou art Lord of all, and there is none that can resist Thy Will" (Esther 13:9). Thou canst produce mature fruits quickly, Thou canst lay foundations late. Say but the word and my soul shall be healed. O Lord, make haste to help me! "Do it for Thy Name's sake" (Jer. 14:7).

"I have regarded My own holy Name....It is not for your sake that I will do this, O house of Israel, but for My holy Name's sake....I will give you a new heart, and put a new spirit within you. And I will take the stony heart out of your flesh and give you a heart of flesh. And I will put My Spirit in the midst of you" (Ezechiel 36:26).

After Communion

"O ye Angels of the Lord, bless the Lord, praise and exalt Him above all for ever" (Dan. 3:58).

"For this is God, our God unto eternity, and for ever and ever" (Ps. 47:15).

"Praise ye the Name of the Lord, O you His servants, you that stand in the house of the Lord, in the courts of the house of our God" (Ps. 134:1).

"O magnify the Lord with me, and let us extol His Name together" (Ps. 33:4).

"For He hath satisfied the empty soul, and hath filled the hungry soul with good things" (Ps. 106:9).

"Give glory to the Lord for He is good, for His mercy endureth for ever" (*Ibid.*).

"Bless the Lord, O my soul, and never forget all He hath done for thee" (Ps. 102:2).

"He raiseth up the soul and enlighteneth the eyes, and giveth health, and life, and blessing" (Ecclus. 34:20).

How hath He not with Himself given us all things!

"Thanks be to God for His unspeakable Gift" (2 Cor. 9:15).

"Lord, I suffer violence, answer for me" (Isa. 38:14). I believe most firmly that Thou art here present. I know that the Master is come and calleth for me. And I am powerless to rouse myself to anything like response. All that faith does is to keep painfully before me what I ought to be and to do. It does not go on to supply the need: it does not lead to worship, and thanksgiving, and love. Effort only tires. Self-reproach irritates and makes things worse. What shall I do, Lord? What is there that I can do?

Lie still before Thee like the poor paralytic on his couch; look wistfully; wait patiently; be glad that Thy glory is not dependent on any exertion or achievement of mine; take comfort from the thought that the physician does not look for entertainment on the part of his patient. He comes to see not what *should be*, but what *is*. O Physician of my soul, I am best seen by Thee at my worst. Thy visit is well timed. Take Thy seat by my bedside; lay my fevered hand in Thine; note how weak I am. Scarcely can I turn my head to look at Thee, or speak a word, or give a smile of welcome. Lord, I suffer violence, answer for me.

The physician questions the nurse. Lord, Thou knowest all things and needest not to ask of any. My soul is the work of Thy hands. Its every disease and infirmity, each flaw, and ache, and sore is known to Thee, better known than to itself. And the sources whence all these spring; the fund of misery that is the fallen creature's heritage; its hidden springs of action; its capabilities; its limitations—all this is known to Thee. "For neither is there any creature invisible in Thy sight, but all things are naked and open to Thine eyes" (Heb. 4:13). If such a One shall answer for us, will not all be well? His knowledge of us is our hope. For we have not a Physician who cannot have compassion on our infirmities. "For He knoweth our frame, He remembereth that we are dust" (Ps. 102:14).

To answer for another is not to ignore or slur over what is faulty, but to make common cause with the defaulter. Do this for me, O merciful Advocate. Stand in my stead; undertake my defence; meet all charges against me. The miserable welcome I give Thee today may be the result of my own wrong-doing or of physical causes; in either case, answer for me. Thou who knowest my frame, who seest what calls for blame in my state, and what for pity—answer for me, find excuse for me. With the sinner Thais I cry to Thee: "Thou who hast made me, have mercy on me."

"What have we to do with Thee, Jesus, Son of the most High God," cried the evil spirit in the synagogue of Capharnaum. It was a wail of despair. The poor ruined creature recognised the presence of God made man, the promised Saviour, but knew that it was not for its sake He had come.

O Jesus, my Saviour, it is for us, it is for me that Thou art here. I have everything to do with Thee. Thou art more to me than father, mother, sister, brother. I am Thy redeemed one, bought with a great price; Thy strayed sheep brought back on Thy shoulders to the fold; Thy friend invited to Thy table, fed with Bread from heaven. Jesus, who to save me was made man and dwelt amongst us; Jesus, who hast loved me even unto the death of the Cross; Jesus, who hast delivered me from the wrath to come—I have everything to do with Thee. Thou art all in all to me. For what have I in heaven, and besides Thee what do I desire upon earth. Thou art the God of my heart, and the God that is my portion forever.

Oblation and Petition, p. 82.

Prayer before a Crucifix, p. 12.

THE WELCOME OF TRUST

THE WELCOME OF TRUST

I

On the Seashore.

Before Communion

IS THERE a more beautiful picture in the Gospels, even in St. Luke's picture Gospel, than the closing scene of St. John's?

The disciples are gathered round our Lord after their miraculous haul of fish. It is on the shore of the Sea of Galilee, that spot rich on every side with memories of their Master. Far into the distance stretches the pebbly beach, recalling their vocation three years ago, when they left all things to follow Him. Yonder, behind the mountains, lies the plain where He fed the hungry multitude. High up is the ledge of rock where He prayed that night of the miracle, the tempest howling round Him. Down those slopes He came to them, and across the stormy waves. Here He had taught from Peter's boat. Here too, once before, He had blessed their fishing, and promised that thenceforth they should catch men.

It is early morning; no one about as yet, save in the distance a few fishermen coming in disappointed after a toilsome night. The seven have Him all to themselves, for since the Resurrection He comes for His friends alone.

The Resurrection—what memories that word awakens! What they have learned since then. They look back upon their three years' companionship with Jesus of Nazareth, and marvel at the Providence of God. The path that so plainly led to Calvary was hidden from them lest they should be scandalised and fall away from Him. He spoke of what was to come, and they understood not. He told them that the Shepherd should be struck, and that the flock would be scattered, and they had met His warnings with vehement protestation. Then the storm had broken over them. It had swept them from His side for a brief space, but His love had sought them, His arm had gathered them again, and here on the seashore they were round Him once more.

All was clear now—how it was meet that Christ should suffer and so enter into His glory; how the disciples must be as their Lord, and through many tribulations enter into the Kingdom of God.

See them, these seven—Peter has swum ashore, and his rough seaman's coat is dripping on the sand. But He is absolutely unconscious of discomfort. His weather-beaten face is aglow with love and enthusiasm as he looks upon the Face of his Master. Not a trace in him of diffidence or depression. Was he not forgiven? Had not the Lord made right the past and restored all he had forfeited? Why should he not rejoice with the innocent, and be foremost in the service still? It was Peter who led out to that night's fishing; he who at John's whispered word: "It is the Lord," had cast himself into the sea with the old eagerness for a secret word before the rest should come. It was he who at his Master's bidding went up and drew the net to land full of great fishes, one hundred and fifty-three. In reward of his profession, not of faith as at Caesarea Philippi, but of love, he is presently to receive the charge of the whole flock, and the promise of a death like to his Lord's whereby to glorify God. Eager, trusting soul, how dear he is to Christ!

Close to him is Thomas. He had missed too much by being parted from Peter to risk separation from him any more. See him feasting eyes and heart on his Lord and his God, for whom in his loyalty he had desired to die.

And Bartholomew, the guileless, fit companion for John.

And John himself, with that far-reaching gaze of his penetrating the mysteries of "the Word of life which was from the beginning, which he had heard, and seen, and handled" (1 John 1:1) with such familiarity in the past. How he marvels at his boldness in laying his head on that breast, at the love that had made him, among the beloved, a the disciple whom Jesus loved."

Feel the freshness of the morning breeze. See the blue Lake; the fire flickering on the strand; the silvery, moving mass of fish; our Lord in His own affectionate way inviting the disciples: "Come and dine;" taking His place among them; helping them. See the awe and bewildered delight with which they gaze on Him and take food from His hand.

Notice in Christ our Lord the marvellous union of the human and the divine. By a word He had filled their nets and provided fire and bread. Now with gentle courtesy He invites them to take refreshment: "Come and dine." "Come," not "Go." "And Jesus cometh and taketh bread and giveth them, and fish in like manner." Is He not determined that they shall acknowledge Him for the same as heretofore? What

wonder that with all their incredulity and hardness of
heart they can no longer deny Him the trust He seeks;
that here on the seashore none of them who are at
meat durst ask Him: "Who art Thou," knowing that
it is the Lord.

When will His lowliness and His sweetness bear
the same fruit in us? When will the urgency of His
invitation bring us as eager guests to His table, our faith
and trust so strong, that in spite of our unworthiness
we have no misgivings, "knowing that it is the Lord?"

Our Divine Brother is "like us in all things"—
yet how unlike! To forgive and forget is a hard task
for us, but look at Him here at meat with the seven.
For three years these men have been His carefully
trained disciples. They have seen His miracles, and
have been themselves entrusted with His miraculous
powers. They have been His confidants and familiar
friends. They declared their readiness to go with
Him to prison and to death. And in the hour of
His need—"they all leaving Him, fled." What
wonder that when He returned to them from the
dead, risen to an immortal life, they should be slow
to believe He could ever be to them as before; that
they looked timidly into His Face to read there what
they might expect. How did He meet that wistful
glance? How did He treat these friends, so frail,

and yet withal so true? With all the tenderness of
His generous self-forgetting Heart. It needed all the
loving ways—nay, more than the affectionateness of
the past—to reassure them. Therefore it was that He
gave to all abundantly, upbraiding not, gave with freer
hand because of their greater need. More than ever
must He identify Himself with them and share with
them all He has. At the Last Supper He had said:
"I will not now call you servants, but I have called you
friends." After the Resurrection they are no longer
friends, but "brethren." "Go to My brethren and say
to them: I ascend to My Father and to your Father, to
My God and your God."

He is the same now; the same with us as with the
seven on the seashore that day; "Jesus Christ yesterday,
to-day, and forever." When the fear of past or of
present infidelity casts us down, let us draw near to that
blessed group by the Lake and see Him seated amid
His brethren, the men who had denied and forsaken
Him. And casting an eye upon the Tabernacle where
He is with us still, hear Him say to us too: "Fear not,
it is I Myself."

After Communion

Whence is this to me that my Lord should come
to me?

"For this is God, our God unto eternity, and for ever and ever" (Ps. 47:15).

Lord, I am not worthy that Thou shouldst enter under my roof.

"Let all Thy works, O Lord, praise Thee, and let Thy saints bless Thee" (Ps. 144:10).

"I will be glad and rejoice in Thee" (Ps. 9:3).

"I will extol Thee, O God my King: and I will bless Thy Name for ever, yea for ever and ever" (Ps. 144:1).

"Give praise to our God, all ye His servants, and you that fear Him, little and great" (Apoc. 19:5).

"Sing to the Lord, O ye His saints" (Ps. 29:5).

"O love the Lord, all ye His saints" (Ps. 30:24).

"Praise ye the Name of the Lord, O you His servants, you that stand in the house of the Lord, in the courts of the house of our God" (Ps. 134:1).

"Praise ye the Lord, for the Lord is good; sing ye to His Name, for it is sweet" (Ps. 134:3).

I thank Thee, O dearest Lord, for all Thou art, all Thou hast been to me. Mine is a longstanding debt. From eternity to eternity Thou art God. From eternity to eternity I have been with Thee, to whom all things are present. I have had a place in Thy designs. I have had focused upon me all the Wisdom, all the Love, of the eternal God. Every circumstance of my life, even to its least detail, has been from eternity chosen by Him, in view of the position in His Court that is to be mine some day, of the place in His Heart that is mine now.

I thank Thee, Lord, for the love with which from eternity Thou didst determine to become man for me; to live a humble life for my example and consolation; to go through Thy cruel Passion, to found Thy Church, to institute Thy Sacraments—for me. To leave the Bosom of the Father and become a wayfarer on earth, would cost Thee much: but Thou couldst pay the price—it was for me. The coldness and ingratitude of men, the scourging, the falling away of Thy friends, the desolation of Thy Blessed Mother, the dereliction on the Cross—all this would be hard to bear, but not too hard—it was for me. Oh, what it would cost to furnish those "Fountains of the Saviour" whence I was to draw with joy; to provide that Table at which I was to be ever a welcome guest! Not with corruptible things, but with the last drop of His Blood was my Redemption to be purchased. I was to be bought with a great price, but He gave it willingly, eagerly, for it was to deliver me from the wrath to come.

And the return? He saw it in Gethsemane, and was made sorrowful even unto death. He saw what

I should account acknowledgment sufficient for all He has done for me. He saw me assisting at His unbloody Sacrifice; He saw the sorrow I bring to the Sacrament of forgiveness; the welcome I give Him in the Sacrament of His love. Was it worth His while to do so much for such return as I should make Him? Yes, so He judged it. I should not be always irresponsive. At last the sense of His loving-kindness would break in upon my soul; I should come to realise something of the value of His unspeakable Gift; I should desire, at least, to return Him love for love. He could wait. He has waited until now.

How long, O Lord, how long? Has not the time come for my heart to make such response as it can to Thine? "O my Lord, let me love Thee, and let the reward of my love be to love Thee daily more and more" (St. Ignatius).

OBLATION

"What shall I offer to the Lord that is worthy?
Wherewith shall I kneel before the high God?"
— Micheas vi.

I have nothing but what is His gift to me. But His own gifts He will accept from my hand as if they were not already His; as if they were something of which

He stands in need, and for the bestowal of which He accounts Himself my debtor. O loving Lord, how immense is Thy condescension to me, Thy needy creature; how tender Thy compassion for me, Thy little child!

I come to Thee, then, with all I have and am. I offer Thee my soul and body, all the good things of this life with which Thou hast blessed me—my family, my friends. My work and my amusements, my responsibilities and my anxieties, my temptations and dangers, my desires and disappointments, all the circumstances and vicissitudes of life, all its trials and its consolations, all my interests for this world and the world to come, my life and my death—I offer them all to Thee, dear Lord.

And since this is still a worthless offering, I gather together and bring to Thee all the glory and praise rendered Thee from the beginning, and to be rendered throughout eternity by any of Thy creatures—the undistracted worship of the Angels; the labours of the Apostles and of missioners to spread the knowledge of Thy Name; the constancy of the Martyrs and of the multitude of meek sufferers who have followed Thee bearing their cross; the patience of the Confessors, and of all who in the ceaseless conflict with self, hold on in spite of weariness and defeat, to the end; all the purity of the Virgins; all the tears of those who have washed their robes and made them white in the Blood of the Lamb. I rejoice in the love and loyalty of these Thy faithful servants, and offer it to Thee in reparation for my coldness and my sloth. I unite in the perfect worship and service of Thy one perfect creature, the Virgin most faithful, loftiest in dignity, lowliest in self-abasement before Thee. I offer Thee the worship that alone is adequate, alone is worthy of Thee— the praise, reverence, and service of Thy Incarnate Son; all the sufferings of His infancy, the privations of His youth, the hardships and persecutions of His manhood, the torments of His Passion, the glory of His Resurrection, His intercession for us in the heavens at Thy right hand, the unspeakable Gift of His Real Presence with us to the end of time, the pure Oblation, the perpetual Sacrifice with its infinite merits offered to Thy Name in every place throughout the world.

Behold, O God our Protector, and look on the Face of Thy Christ. How have we not also with Him given Thee all things?

PETITION

"If thou didst know the Gift of God!"

"O child, did you but know the power you have now over My Heart, you would do it a holy violence, you would wrest from Me the grace that the violent bear away. You would save sinners who are going to refuse their last grace. You would rescue the little children whose parents have given them over to be slain. You would place at once in heaven the souls that are crying for your pity and your help. You would strengthen the hands and cheer the hearts of My dearly loved missioners who carry My Name to those who know Me not. You would win the light of faith for those who are seeking it, and strength for those who have found the treasure but lack courage to sell all they have to purchase it. If you knew what I have done for you in giving you Myself, if you had faith as a grain of mustard seed, you would stretch out your hand to strong things. To the uttermost parts of the earth, and beyond the earth, into the dreary land of Purgatory, wherever redeemed souls are to be saved and helped, the fruits of your Communion would reach."

I wish, O Lord, that I could open Thy way into every heart, that I could put the keys of every fortress over the wide earth into Thy hands. But they are there already. Not only the keys of death and hell, but the key to every human heart is in Thy keeping. All its complex wards Thou knowest; the rust of years that makes ingress difficult is no bar to Thee.

Every difficulty yields to Thy touch. Thou holdest the key, O Lord—nay, Thou art Thyself the key. "O key of David, who openest, and no one shutteth; shuttest, and no one openeth; come, and deliver from prison the fettered sitting in darkness and in the shade of death."

I pray to Thee for all who are mine, all whom Thou hast given me to love and care for. May my Communion be their safeguard and their growth in grace today. May it be light, and strength, and consolation to our holy Father, the Pope, to all bishops and priests, to all who are striving to win souls to Thee, to the poor, the suffering, the tempted, the little children. May its grace flow through the Church like the river of the water of life through the Heavenly Jerusalem, and let its fruits be the healing of the nations. Let it flow to every soul outside the unity of the visible Church, to my relatives and friends, to the poor heathen beyond the reach of sacramental grace. O Jesus, my heart sinks at the thought of the nine hundred millions of redeemed souls that now, in this twentieth century, have not as yet heard their Saviour's Name! Send forth labourers into the vineyard and bring to Thy knowledge and Thy love these multitudes bought with Thy Precious Blood. They say that Teresa won to Thee as many souls as Francis Xavier. The need of intercessory prayer has not lessened since her day, and if there are not now Saints enough to move Thy mercy, what canst Thou do, O Lord, but hear the prayers of sinners? Hear my prayer, it has more than the efficacy of a Saint's today, it is Thine own, for Thou art mine.

O Heart of Christ, Ark of the perishing world, to Thee all the elect are fleeing for safety from the wrath of God and the torrents of iniquity that cover the earth. Draw into Thy shelter, not only those who seek it, but those that seek it not and need it most. Thou wert opened on Calvary to admit us all, and through all time Thou remainest open, that all who will may be saved by Thee. When the last of the elect shall have entered into salvation by Thee, the door will be closed and the wrath of God descending will consume all not found therein.

O Heart of Jesus, salvation of those who trust in Thee, have mercy on us! Heart of Jesus that hast delivered us from the wrath to come, draw all men to Thee, compel them to come in that the number of the saved may be multiplied. Wherever there is temptation to be overcome, innocence to be guarded, death to be met by sea or by land, final perseverance to be assured, the good to be supported, the weak to be strengthened, the fallen to be raised, the sad to be comforted—there let the fruit of my Communion be!

Prayer before a Crucifix, p. 12.

THE WELCOME OF TRUST

II

"If He delay, wait for Him"—Hab. 2:3.

66 "I WISH our Lord were more to me," we often say or think. Who does not wish this? "Who is there," says à Kempis, "that would not willingly receive comfort, if he could always have it?" But these heavenly visitations are few and far between. We could not be trusted with them often. God sometimes gives them plentifully, twice in a spiritual course—at the beginning, when the soul first turns to Him and has to be enticed into the narrow way of self-conquest; and towards the close of the journey if it has been brave and, so to speak, merited a reward. But with the most of us, perhaps, as with our predecessors in the desert, "God is not well pleased." There is no

particular reason why He should treat us as favourites, nor is there anything very special to reward. Hence, having got us safely into the way of salvation, He gives us abundantly all needful help, puts up with our niggardly service, sets right our mistakes, forgives our many lapses, and bears with us patiently when we cry out to Him for consolation and sweetness.

"You know not what you ask," He says to us at times, as to James and John. "Could you see your labour as I see it, you would be ashamed to ask for more than your promised penny. You would see, too, that what you ask would not be good for you, that it is safer and better to leave yourself in My hands, and like a well-behaved child take what is given you without wanting something else." We notice that in the prayer our Lord has put into our mouth He bids us ask for all that is necessary for soul and body, not for dainties: "Give us this day our daily bread," not "bread and butter."

Through the grace of adoption and the merits of our Elder Brother, we are "followers of God as most dear children" (Eph. 5:1). But it will help us, when we feel inclined to grumble, to remember what we are of ourselves, what our sins deserve. "We indeed justly receive the due reward of our deeds," said the good thief. Which of us cannot say as much when troubles come, or the monotony of the daily tramp makes us sigh for the sense of His Presence whose companionship brightens the darkest and the dullest road? "When Jesus is present all goes well and nothing seems difficult, but when Jesus is absent everything is hard" (Imitation. 2. 8).

What can we do but brace ourselves to patience? It will not be always thus, and whether there be more of punishment or of simple trial in the present state of things, it will not last—our time of probation is coming to an end, and that soon: "For yet a little and a very little while, and He that is to come, will come, and will not delay" (Heb. 10:37).

Meanwhile, let us look our difficulty fairly in the face.

I am never tired of bemoaning the difficulties of prayer. I contrast conversation with God with the face-to-face intercourse, the response of eye and lip and ear that makes converse with a friend so precious and so helpful.

But do I look at the other side, am I fair to prayer? The most sympathetic of friends cannot penetrate far into my soul, cannot change the circumstances of life that are troubling it, or its attitude towards those circumstances. But the Friend to whom I speak in prayer sounds my soul to its depths. His eye follows its windings into recesses that I do not even suspect. He sees the effect of every subtle influence upon it. He analyses every trouble. He can remove the cause, or soften its effect upon me, or brace me to bear and profit by it. He can work a change in my inmost being, in my views of life, in my estimate of success and failure, of position, influence, family or spiritual trials. He can supplement the deficiencies of my character. He can satisfy every aspiration of my mind, every need of my heart. When I lay my pain before Him with: "Lord, Thou knowest," I bring to bear upon that pain all the Omniscience and Omnipotence of God, all, and infinitely more than all, the fellow-feeling of the most devoted of human friends. Is not this a set-off against the unsatisfactoriness of prayer of which I complain?

Lord, could I bring myself to think more of the inestimable boon Thou hast given me in prayer, than of what by the nature of things I cannot have as yet, how different my prayer would be! My heart would be always lifting itself to Thee in thankfulness and trust. I should accept humbly the obscurities and limitations of this time of faith. But faith would grow to be so bright, and trust would win from Thee such abundant reward even here, that the veil would be half lifted. Prayer would come to be my resource and my delight. Thy injunction, "Pray always," would seem to be the most natural thing in the world. Like Thy first followers, my conversation would be in heaven.

Thou, the Lord of heaven, art coming to hold converse with me today. Thou comest in the very flesh that lay in the manger and on the cross, Body and Blood, Soul and Divinity, Thy Sacred Humanity entire. But without its accidents or appearances. I have to content myself with the substance. I have to stay my soul on the realities revealed to faith, till the day breaks and the shadows retire.

So, too, with myself. I come to Thee with the necessary dispositions, my soul in friendship with Thee. Yet without the accessories of sensible fervour which I desire, it may be, more for my own sake than for Thine. But what of this? Feelings are but accidents. I must have patience till the veils drop and I see the King in His beauty. Then shall I be glad with exceeding joy. Then shall my soul magnify the Lord indeed, and my spirit rejoice in God my Saviour. Then all that is within me shall praise His holy Name.

I shall be satisfied when Thy glory shall appear. But there is no harm in pleading for a little lifting of the veil from time to time for a few crumbs from Thy table, O tender and compassionate Lord. I could not disappoint the dumb creatures that come to me

trustfully for food or a caress—the dog that looks up
into my face, the bird that alights on my hand. Thou
hast told me that I am of much more value than these.
Wilt Thou, then, disappoint me when I come to Thee
for the food my soul needs, for the grace I must have if
I am to reach heaven? Wilt Thou not now and then
give me the caress for which I look, Thou who hast
said: "Upon the knees you shall be caressed. As one
whom the mother caresseth, so will I comfort you?"
(Isa. 66:13) Wilt Thou not speak at times that secret
word in my soul which thrills it through and through?
"My soul melted when my Beloved spake," says the
bride in the Canticles. Speak to me, my Beloved, and
melt the hardness of my heart.

"Hear my prayer, O Lord, and my supplication:
give ear to my tears" (Ps. 38:13).

"Who giveth food to the young ravens that call
upon Thee" (Ps. 146:9).

"Thou, Lord, art rich enough to give me much
more than this" (2 Par. 25:9).

"Can the rush be green without moisture?"
(Job 8:11).

"Remember me, O my God, unto good. Amen"
(2 Esdras 13:31).

"And He gave them their request, and sent fullness
into their souls" (Ps. 105:15).

After Communion

"My Lord and my God."

"Lord, I believe; help Thou my unbelief."

"Lord, increase my faith."

"O Lord, there is none like Thee; let Thy name be magnified for ever" (1 Par. 17:24).

"The Lord is my Helper and my Protector: in Him hath my soul confided, and I have been helped" (Ps. 27:7).

"Sing to the Lord, O ye His Saints" (Ps. 29:5).

"O love the Lord, all ye His Saints" (Ps. 30:24).

"For He hath satisfied the empty soul, and hath filled the hungry soul with good things" (Ps. 106:9).

"Blessed be the Lord, for He hath shown His wonderful mercy to me" (Ps. 30:22).

"Thanks be to God for His unspeakable Gift" (2 Cor. 9:15).

"One is good, God" (Matt. 19:17).

How near I am now—nay, how closely united I am now, to the Source of all good. I cross my hands upon my breast and know that, folded there, is all good. For "One is good, God."

And He is here to share with me, like a true lover, all that He has and is. Within my breast is:—

All His Omnipotence to protect me—"Thou shalt know that the Lord thy God is a strong and faithful God" (Deut. 7:9).

All His Wisdom to guide me—"Abide thou with Me, fear not" (1 Kings 22:23).

All His loving-kindness to help me—"I will not leave thee nor forsake thee" (Jos. 1:5).

All His charity to warm me—"Our God is a consuming fire" (Heb. 12:29).

All His zeal to enkindle mine, for "The charity of Christ presseth us" (2 Cor. 5:14).

All His treasures to enrich me, for "He that spared not even His own Son . . . how hath He not also with Him given us all things!" (Rom. 8:32).

All His merits to plead for me—"Ever living to make intercession for us" (Heb. 7:25).

Out of Thee, my God, there is no good. And within Thee there is no good that is not Thyself. All that Thou hast Thou art. Therefore in asking Thee for all I need for my soul's health, I ask for Thyself. Thou art Thyself the light, the strength, the love, the patience, the holiness, that are wanting to me. How near to me is all this in the supremely precious moments after Communion! Not at my door, not within my reach, but absolutely within my breast. Open, then, Thy hand to me, O Lord, and fill Thy needy creature with benediction by filling it with Thyself.

O Infinite Beauty that art my God, I praise Thee.

O Infinite Charity that art my God, I love Thee.

O Infinite Patience that art my God, I thank Thee.

O Infinite Goodness that art my God, I worship Thee, and bless Thee, and cling to Thee now and forever.

Dear Master, I am like Magdalen at Thy feet. Would that I could be like her in her warm welcome, in her loving content, in her attentive listening as Thou didst speak to her heart, in the concentration of all the powers of her soul upon Thee as long as Thou remainedst her Guest, in her sympathy with Thy sorrows, in the consolation she brought to Thy Heart. Can I, with my wandering thoughts and my coldness, be to Thee in any measure like Magdalen? Yes, for Thou hast told us Thou wilt accept desires as acts. When at the Last Supper Thou didst pray for Thy Apostles, and not for them only, but for those who through their word should believe in Thee, Thou knewest that these later disciples would have difficulties unknown to those whom the charm of Thy divine Person drew to Thee during Thy life on earth. We have not met Thy glance nor heard the tones of Thy voice, nor listened to the words of Him who spake as never man spake. We have the record of the impression made on the crowds and on those who loved Thee, but we have yet to come under that spell ourselves. Meanwhile, Thou hast compassion on us, knowing that faith which does so much cannot do all. Often, too, faith itself is withdrawn into the innermost recesses of the soul. It is like the sap of the plant in winter: no fruit, nor flower, nor bud betrays its presence. But it is there. Thine eye can see it, and Thou hast patience.

What advice hast Thou for us till the sun comes forth in his strength and vivifies the plant and draws out its hidden energies, till winter is over and gone, and the flowers appear in our land? Thou wouldst have us betake ourselves to our brethren who are better off than we are; whose vehement desires go forth to meet Thee; whose hearts glow in Thy presence; whose whole being even to the restless senses is subdued and captivated by Thy sacramental touch; whose entertainment of their Divine Guest, while it remains infinitely unworthy of Him, is so true a welcome that He makes it His delight to be with them. By the Communion of Saints they are our brethren; their riches are the property of all, and the poorest members of the family can help themselves at will. Thou dost not ask if the gifts we offer Thee are our own or borrowed. But Thou dost accept them graciously, make much of them, account them of great worth. I offer to Thee, then, dear Lord, the unspotted purity of Thy virgins and of all innocent souls: the fortitude of Thy martyrs who are upholding Thy cause in the midst of tortures and death; the patience of Thy confessors and of all who are serving Thee amid persecution and pain, or in the monotonous round of daily duties and trials. I offer Thee that immaculate heart in which Thou findest every virtue in its perfection. I offer Thee Thy own Sacred Human Heart, whose worship and praise is worthy of the divine acceptance. Thanks be to Thee for this rich treasury to which I may come for the supply of all my need. Thanks, above all, for the Divine Heart which alone suffices for me. Thanks be to God for His unspeakable Gift!

Petition, p. 102.

Prayer before a Crucifix, p. 12.

THE WELCOME OF TRUST

III

*"Cast thy care upon the Lord, and
He shall sustain thee"*—Ps. 54:23.

BEFORE COMMUNION

66 "FOR he stands at too great a hazard that does not cast his whole care on Thee" (Imitation iii. 17). How different from ours is this way of putting things! We should have said the hazard was in casting our whole care on God. Of course we trust Him perfectly, but there is such a thing as prudence, and one cannot help being uneasy when trouble threatens, or difficulties arise, or things go wrong. A certain amount of care, quite enough to justify solicitude, disquietude even, is unavoidable. Thus do we petulantly turn our back upon the invitation and the promise of God, as if it meant nothing and

was never intended to have any practical bearing on our conduct.

Yet how strong are our Lord's words: "Therefore I say to you, be not solicitous for your life, what you shall eat, nor for your body what you shall put on. . . . Behold the birds of the air, for they neither sow, nor do they reap, nor gather into barns: and your Heavenly Father feedeth them. Are not you of much more value than they? And for raiment why are you solicitous? Consider the lilies of the field how they grow: they labour not, neither do they spin. . . . And if the grass of the field God doth so clothe, how much more you, O ye of little faith? Be not solicitous therefore, saying, What shall we eat, or wherewith shall we be clothed? For your Father knoweth that you have need of all these things. Be not therefore solicitous for tomorrow. Seek first the Kingdom of God, and His justice, and all these things shall be added unto you" (Matt. 6:25).

How He insists! Not even about the most fundamental needs, for the bare necessaries of life are we to be solicitous. He prefaces His injunction by the solemn words: "I say to you." I who cannot deceive, nor bid you trust too much, I bid you be not solicitous. Why? Because "your Father knoweth your need."

There are those who take Him at His word. They omit nothing that depends on them. They do what is

not required of the lilies and the birds; they toil and
they spin. Like the "wise steward whom his lord set
over his family to give them wheat in due season"; like
the valiant woman "who looked well to the ways of
her house"; they do all that in them lies. And then,
obedient to the Divine injunction, and relying on the
Divine promise, they cast all their care upon God.
"The Lord ruleth me and I shall want nothing" (Ps.
22:1). "My God is my Helper; in Him will I put my
trust" (Ps. 17:3). Who shall tell the peace of such
souls, the wonderful interventions in their favour, the
vigilance with which He whom their trust glorifies
provides for their every need!

A rower propels his boat by a twofold impulse,
a movement forward and back. So do we advance
towards God. We tend to Him by desire and affection,
and fall back upon Him by self-abandonment and
trust. And it is in the latter act that our progress
chiefly lies.

My God, give me such trust in Thee that I may be
able to take literally Thy words: "Be not solicitous."
Let not the cares of this life so weigh upon me as to
trouble my peace. Give me the filial trust that Thy
blessed Apostle Paul laid as a duty on Thy first
disciples: "Be nothing solicitous, but in everything
by prayer and supplication let your petitions be

made known to God. And the peace of God which surpasseth all understanding keep your hearts and minds in Christ Jesus" (Philipp. 4:6).

Give me the peaceful heart of Thy dear Foster-Father amid the ups and downs of life, the obscurity shrouding Divine designs, the peril threatening the treasures confided to him. To him the Will of God was all in all. It was impulse; it was rest. It was the reason and the justification of all things. It was compensation in suffering, and goal beyond which he had no desire. Nothing came amiss to him; every trial, however sudden, or grievous, or prolonged, found him ready, as if it had been a plan of his own devising, long foreseen and thought out in every detail, as if it fell in exactly with his wishes. And so indeed it did, inasmuch as it was the ordering or the permission of God's Providence, a fresh revelation of the Divine plan. O Prince of Peace, who hast brought to earth a peace that no trial can disturb, come to my troubled heart, say to it: "Peace, be still!"

"In Thee, Lord, I put my trust" (Ps. 10:2).

"It is good for me to adhere to my God, to put my trust in the Lord God" (Ps. 72:28).

"The Lord ruleth me, and I shall want nothing" (Ps. 22:1).

"For though I should walk in the midst of the shadow of death, I will fear no evils, for Thou art with me" (Ps. 22:4).

"I have cried to the Lord, and the Lord will save me" (Ps. 54:17).

"In Thee, O Lord, have I hoped, let me never be confounded" (Ps. 30:2).

AFTER COMMUNION

"Bless the Lord, all ye servants of the Lord" (Ps. 133:1).

"Exalt ye the Lord our God" (Ps. 98:5).

"Bless the Lord, all ye His Angels" (Ps. 102:20).

"Give glory to the Lord, for He is good" (Ps. 106:1).

"Adore the Lord our God, and give thanks to Him" (Tobias 11:7).

"Adore the Lord my God" (Dan. 14:24).

"Bless the Lord, for He hath shown His wonderful mercy to me" (Ps. 30:22).

"For He hath satisfied the empty soul, and hath filled the hungry soul with good things" (Ps. 106:9).

"My soul doth magnify the Lord, and my spirit hath rejoiced in God my Saviour" (Luke 1:46).

"Because He that is mighty hath done great things to me, and holy is His Name" (Luke 1:49).

My God, who hast given Thyself to me with all that Thou hast and art, with reason dost Thou expect me to trust Thee. Thou art my Father, and I am never to question Thy love and care. All my life is planned by Thee, Infinite Wisdom and Infinite Love guiding the arrangement of its every detail. The ordering of Thy Providence has my welfare in view as completely as if I alone were to be considered. I am not sacrificed to others as is so often the case in the affairs of this life when the designer is one of ourselves. The paths of Thy children cross and re-cross at an infinite number of points; circumstances appear to be the most absolute result of chance. But every contact, every event even the most trivial, even the result of the free-will and the ill-will of man, is ordered or permitted by Thee. Reaching from end-to-end mightily is Thy loving foresight, ordering all things sweetly for the child of Thy Heart—all things, all things without exception, those even that seem most opposed to my good. Let not such things take me by surprise or disconcert me. Say to me as to Peter: "Go with them, doubting nothing, for I have sent them" (Acts 10:20). Let me put my hand trustfully into Thine and keep it there all through the changing years, believing by faith what I shall see some day: "He hath done all things well." With what admiration and delight shall I behold in eternity the Divine skill which has shaped to Thy designs all the varied elements of life—talents, deficiencies, pleasure, pain, temptation, failure, falls— all things working together to my final good. "He hath done all things well," I shall cry out in exulting praise, "He hath done all things well."

Could there be any cloud in that happy retrospect, any note of sadness in that praise, it would be where my trust failed during life, where the things that *seem* obscured the bright realities that faith should have kept visible through every trial.

O my Father, my Heavenly Father, give me this birthright of Thy children, this abounding hope, this grace of trust. Care for me as for a child that lies without thought for itself in its father's arms. Care for me till I come to see Thee, O God of my life, to know Thee as Thou art, to love Thee with every affection of my heart, to spend my eternity before Thy face in jubilant praise.

"O Lord, Father, and God of my life" (Ecclus. 23:4), everywhere and in all things Thou art "God blessed for ever" (Rom. 9:5). Yet Thou hast a special nearness to me and dearness as the God of my life, whose character is disclosed to me, not by any revelation from without, but by the intimate experience of daily life—daily trials, daily joys and sorrow, and unexpected intervention, and sweet surprise, and tender consolation. O Lord, Father, and God of my life, let me give Thee that worship which is so acceptable to Thee, the worship to which the experience of long years entitles Thee—the trust of a child.

Obation and Petition, p. 10.

Prayer before a Crucifix, p. 12.

THE WELCOME OF A HOST

THE WELCOME OF A HOST

I

*"He came unto His own,
and His own received Him not"*—John 1:11.

BEFORE COMMUNION

THUS the disciple whom Jesus loved begins his Gospel. He who knew the Sacred Heart better than the others, who had leaned on his Master's breast and learned His secrets—it is he who tells us of the chief suffering of that loving Heart in the days when pain could reach it.

Who came? He who had been so long promised. He who was so sorely needed. He who was God, able to supply every need. He who was most eager to free us from our enemies, to save us, to make us happy— He came.

To whom? "To His own." To the people He had

singled out from all others to be His in a special way. On whom He had heaped His favours. Whom He had guided, protected, fed, taught, worked wonders for, loved, warned, promised Himself to. To the chosen people who had sighed for Him, and boasted of Him as one of their race. To these, His own, He came.

How did He come? Not with the pomp and unapproachableness of a king of this world, not imposing heavy burdens—but lowly and meek. As the Good Shepherd, carrying the lambs in His bosom, feeding His flock in rich pastures, seeking that which was lost, binding up that which was broken, strengthening that which was weak; as a Physician, as a Friend, as a Fellow-Traveller, as a Brother—thus He came to His own. He came to share their nature that they might be partakers of His. He came to give them all they were able to receive—peace in this life, happiness even in the midst of sorrow, Himself beneath the veils. And in the next life a happiness perfect and eternal, flowing from the face-to-face vision that fulfills every desire. Thus He came to His own.

With what result? "His own received Him not."

Why? Because they wanted impossibilities. They would be healed without submission to the Physician. They would enjoy the favours of God as His children without leaving the sins that made them His enemies.

They looked for a Messiah who, by heaping upon them the riches, pleasures, and honours of this world, would chain their hearts to the things of time and make them lose those of eternity. He loved them too much to give them what they sought. And thus, when He came unto His own, His own received Him not.

What He sought was a welcome. What we gave Him was a cross. What we give Him still in return for the unspeakable Gift of His abiding Presence with us, is indifference and neglect. He wanders up and down the world, outcast from many a heart.

"Behold, I stand at the door and knock."

Lord, read always over my door "Welcome!" Weary and footsore, come in and rest with me. My house is poor and unfurnished, but at Thy service always. I will give Thee water for Thy feet, the tears of true contrition; spikenard for Thy head, the fragrance at least of humility and good desires. Above all, I will give Thee the kiss of welcome. Come to me and use all that belongs to me as it shall please Thee. I make Thee welcome to anything of mine that it may please Thee to take, to any loss, or sacrifice, or failure; for any humiliation, or pain of body or mind, from now to the hour of my death.

"So long a time have I been with you,
and have you not known Me?" (John 14:9).

This, as the world's history rolls on, is His reproach to its children of each generation. Not to the untaught millions of heathendom whom the glad tidings of the Incarnation and of the Real Presence have never reached, who live and die without having heard of their Saviour, or having once found their way to His feet. Nor to the thousands around His tabernacles whose eyes the prejudices of birth and education have held. But to those whom He has called out of darkness, who see what kings and prophets desired to see, for whom are His teaching and His Sacraments, His continual inspirations and invitations, His morning Sacrifice, His evening Benediction, whose doors lie within a stone's throw of His own. It is to these He says year after year: "So long have I been with you, and have you not known Me?" It is to me, His friend and His familiar, that His reproach is made.

"So long have I been with you." How long is it since He has been within my reach for daily Mass, for frequent Communion?

"And you have not known Me." This can be the only explanation of my neglect of Him. If I knew Him

better, knew the tenderness of His love for me, His eagerness to be with me, His devotedness, I could not keep away from Him as I do. If I knew His interest in all that concerns me, I should find my way to Him oftener with my troubles and my cares.

Welcome, Divine Guest, welcome today! Awaken within my heart some better response to Thine. It is not meet that all the ardour should be on the side of Him who comes, that the host should be so little in accord with the Guest. Come, and bring my heart into harmony with Thine.

When we desire very eagerly the visit of a friend, we are not content with one invitation. We send telegram after telegram. We show we can take no refusal. We even seem inconsiderate, and risk wearying by importunity. We leave our friend no choice. He has to satisfy us at last. "He would not for a long time. But afterwards he said within himself: Because she is troublesome to me I will . . . lest continually coming she weary me" (Luke 18:4). Lord, I desire Thy Blessed Presence with me today. I am not worthy of it, but I beg, I importune, I multiply invitations:—

"Come into my garden" (Cant. 5:1).

"Come, my Beloved" (Cant. 7:11).

"Come, let us see one another" (2 Par. 25:17).

"Come home with me, and I will make Thee presents" (3 Kings 13:7).

"Come, Lord Jesus" (Apoc. 22:20).

AFTER COMMUNION

"My soul doth magnify the Lord, and my spirit hath rejoiced in God my Saviour."

"For He that is mighty hath done great things for me, and holy is His Name."

"O ye Angels of the Lord, bless the Lord: praise and exalt Him above all forever" (Dan. 3:58).

"Come, let us praise the Lord with joy, let us joyfully sing to God our Saviour" (Ps. 94:1).

"Give glory to the Lord for He is good, for His mercy endureth for ever. Who shall declare the power of the Lord! Who shall set forth all His praises!" (Ps. 105:1).

"Let the mercies of the Lord give glory to Him, and His wonderful works to the children of men" (Ps. 106:8).

"Let all Thy works, O Lord, praise Thee, and let Thy Saints bless Thee" (Ps. 144:10).

"I will praise Thee, O Lord, with my whole heart" (Ps. 137:1).

"I will extol Thee, O God my King, and I will bless Thy Name for ever, yea for ever and ever" (Ps. 144:1).

Whence is this to me that my Lord should come to me?

We should not dare to invite a king into a miserable hovel. And were he to invite himself, we should be on thorns the whole time of his stay. Is it want of faith, dear Lord, that makes the case so different when there is question of a visit from Thee? Now and then, when the dignity of my Guest is borne home to me more than usual, there is a thrill of wondering awe or of glad surprise. But my normal feeling is little more than the appreciation of the kindness of a friend who looks in upon me from next door. I take it as a matter of course. I bid Him welcome certainly, but even this bit of courtesy He is expected to take for granted. If He comes on business we draw our chairs together and set to work to discuss it without loss of time. Is it want of faith, O best of friends, that makes me treat Thee with so little ceremony? No doubt the fault is mine in part. But—may I say it with all reverence—is it not also Thine, the natural consequence of Thy accessibility, of the trust with which Thou dost make Thyself over to us? So far from showing any repugnance to visit me in my poverty, Thy courtesy is too delicate to let it appear a condescension. "Behold, I stand at the gate and knock. If any man shall hear My voice and open to Me the door, I will come in to him and will sup with him, and he with Me. My delights are to be with the children of men. Open to Me, My sister, My beloved." What wonder that the unfeigned desire testified by these words should make me lose sight of the infinite distance between us. Whose fault is it, then, dear Lord? If blame is due, must we not share it?

But from another point of view the failing is wholly mine. If Thy gracious ways dull the sense of obligation, they should surely inflame love. And this is Thy design in making Thyself so easy of approach. The human longing to be with Thy friend makes Thee ready at all hours to come to me. But where is my response? Where is the desire of my heart to be with Thee? Thy love cannot be satisfied without my co-operation. From Heaven to the altar-rails is Thy part of the journey. From my bed to the church is mine. How often do I find the way too long, the sacrifice too great! How often do I fail at the rendezvous, and by an indifference, amounting almost to insult, deprive Thee of the meeting on which Thy Heart is set! Is there, then, nothing in me that responds to Thy advances? This at least there is—shame and sorrow for my callousness, and a desire to make up to Thee for the past.

I have within my breast the Heart that loved me uninterruptedly throughout the three-and-thirty years. As the Babe lay on the manger straw; as the Boy lay awake at night in the cottage at Nazareth; as the Man worked hard all day in the village shop; as He preached and cured; as He walked up and down the land, His Heart was beating always with love of me. Slower and slower, as the three hours dragged on, it beat upon the cross, faltering, failing—until it stopped. For part of three days it ceased to beat for me. With the breaking of the dawn on Easter Day, when it woke to an immortal life, it began to beat anew for me. And for nineteen hundred years since then it has never ceased to beat for me, till this morning brings it with its faithful love into my breast.

For what does my heart beat? What is its main concern in life, its absorbing interest? Thou shalt love the Lord thy God with thy whole heart. Thus has the Lord my God loved me. Is it too much to give Him my whole heart in exchange for His?

O Lord, help me, make haste to help me. Had I the power over my heart that Thou hast, I would pour into it an affection answering in some measure to Thine own. I would break down every obstacle to the free flowing of mutual love. I would not suffer devotedness and generosity to be on one side alone. When wilt Thou do for me, O Lord, what I cannot do for myself; when wilt Thou add to Thy gifts the grace to love Thee as I desire?

"Judea disowned Thee for her King, that I might have Thee all my own," said the loving St. Gertrude. "My King and my God" (Ps. 5:3), I choose and proclaim Thee now within my heart. As if Thou were not King by right; as if I were free to elect Thee or not; as if I had not chosen Thee again and again, I choose Thee now. Reign over all that I am and have—over my memory and my imagination, over my understanding and my will, over all my senses. Reign over my thoughts, and desires, and actions. Control and direct every movement of soul and body, every word of my lips, every labour of my hands, every step of my feet, that all may tend to Thy glory and be conformed to Thy will.

Reign over all that is dear to me and dependent on me, over my family and every member thereof. I consecrate each one to Thee, and as far as in me lies subject all to Thy sway. Look upon it, O Lord, as a special and cherished province of Thy Kingdom. Make it loyal to Thee, obedient to Thy laws, eager to carry out Thy good pleasure and to promote Thy glory.

Oblation and Petition, pp. 160, 162.

Prayer before a Crucifix, p. 12.

THE WELCOME OF A HOST

II

"Come."

A BRILLIANT sunrise attracts our eyes to the East and makes us think of the effulgence that will be there one day. What will be the splendour of those heavens that are to gather together and immeasurably to surpass in one last blaze of glory all the magnificence of sunrise and sunset that earth has seen: which are to be lit up by the forms of myriads upon myriads of glorified beings, Angels and men; by the presence of the Son of Man coming in great power and majesty!

How often at sunrise and sunset now do we picture to ourselves that scene. It is the summing up of the world's history, the revelation and justification of every dealing of God with mankind and with each single soul, the manifestation before the whole human race of every thought, word, and deed, since Adam first drew breath in Paradise.

And yet that scene will be a very simple one. All its magnificence, all that array of heaven and earth will find its purport in two words: "Depart" and "Come." To hear those words will heaven be emptied and all mankind assembled in the valley of Jehoshaphat. We tremble as we reflect that the words are only two. There is no *via media* between the path of glory upward and the road down to the abyss. "He that is not with Me is against Me," will be plain upon that day. We think of ourselves, and we tremble. Oh, for some assurance that all will be well with us then, that the word spoken in the hearing of earth and heaven to our individual soul will be the invitation: "Come!" Is such guarantee vouchsafed to us, and if so, where is it to be found?

"Behold I set forth in your sight a blessing and a curse" (Deut. 11:26). "I have set before thee life and good, and on the other hand death and evil" (Deut. 30:15). "As thou shalt choose, and whither it shall please thee to go, thither go" (Jer. 40:4).

"I have chosen the way of truth" (Ps. 118:30).

"Destruction is thy own, O Israel" (Osee 13:9).

"We have in ourselves the answer of death" (2 Cor. 1:9). And of life also.

Those words: "Depart" and "Come," which will be the sentence of death or of life to every one of us, are the result of our deliberate choice during our time of probation. There are those whose abiding disposition is a desire to rid themselves of the presence and of the recollection of God. "Who have said to God: Depart from us, we desire not the knowledge of Thy ways" (Job 21:14). "And behold, the whole city went out to meet Jesus, and when they saw Him they besought Him that He would depart from their coasts" (Matt. 8:34).

And there are those whose lives are spent in the quest of Him, "seeking God and desirous to find Him" (Wisd. 13:6). "Have you seen Him whom my soul loveth?" (Cant. 3:3). "My soul hath desired Thee in the night, and in the morning early I will watch to Thee" (Isa. 26:9). "Show me Thy face, and let Thy voice sound in my ears" (Cant. 2:14). "Come, my Beloved" (Cant. 7:11). "Come, Lord Jesus" (Apoc. 22:20).

Let me, O Lord, be one of these longing ones. Let my soul pant for Thee as the hart for the waterbrooks, and dread, above all evils, separation from Thee. Like the sisters of Bethany let me count it the greatest of blessings to have Thee often under my roof. Like Zaccheus let me receive Thee with joy. And may the echo of my many welcomes during life be that word of Thine to me from the eastern heavens: "Come."

Come. Let this word of invitation to Thee, dearest Lord, be often on my lips and always in my heart.

Come in Thy visitations of mercy and even of justice; for it is Thyself always; Thy disguise but thinly veils Thee, and Faith is ever ready to leap forth to meet Thee, crying: "It is the Lord!"

Come in the secret promptings of Thy grace, in the warnings, the rebukes, the compensations, the caresses, and all the myriad forms love is wont to take.

Come in the lessons of detachment that sooner or later the heart must learn, in the disillusioning, the separations, the loneliness that come with years. Take for Thyself each vacant place, till at last the whole is Thine and Thou art all in all.

Come in Thy Sacramental Presence to claim Thy rights, to give of Thy fullness, to answer prayer, to calm my fears, to purify and draw to Thyself all the affections of my soul.

Come, daily Bread, to sustain me in the journey of each day, as the manna of old strengthened the travellers in the desert for the labour and the monotony of the daily march.

Come in seasons of darkness and distress, when the soul, loosed from her moorings, troubled and storm-swept, is driven for awhile before the blast.

Come when she feels for Thee in the darkness, and cries for Thee as a babe for its mother's face.

Come, above all, in the dreariness and the dangers of death. When all things fall away, stay with me, O Lord. When none other can help or comfort, fold me in the everlasting arms, hide me in Thy Heart. May my last word be that of John the beloved: "Come, Lord Jesus." And may Thy answer be: "Behold, I come quickly." Let my first sight on the eternal shore be "Jesus Christ, mild and festive in aspect," coming to meet me; and the first sound, Thy word, the echo of my own during life: "Come, blessed of My Father—Come!"

AFTER COMMUNION

"Thanks be to God for His unspeakable Gift" (2 Cor. 9:15).

"For this is God, our God unto eternity, and for ever and ever" (Ps. 47:15).

"Bless the Lord, O my soul, and never forget all He hath done for thee" (Ps. 102:2).

"For this is God, our God unto eternity, and for ever and ever."

"Give praise to our God, all ye His servants, and you that fear Him, little and great" (Apoc. 19:5).

"For this is God, our God unto eternity, and for ever and ever."

"O magnify the Lord with me, and let us extol His Name together" (Ps. 33:4).

"For this is God, our God unto eternity, and for ever and ever."

"This is your hour" (Luke 22:53).

Christ. To My enemies who drew near to lead Me to torments and to death, I said as I delivered Myself into their hands: This is your hour. To you, My friend, who invite Me to your heart, I say also, say lovingly: This is your hour.

All the hours of your life are yours, to work in, to traffic with, to use for My glory, for the salvation and perfection of your own soul and the souls of others. All are yours. Yet of the time spent with Me, in My close company after Communion, I say to you as of no other: This is your hour.

It passes quickly; take heed that it passes not without fruit, that its graces are not forfeited, that its privileges are not neglected, that its opportunities are not lost.

This is *your hour*—the hour when you may pay to Me all your debts of adoration, thanksgiving, propitiation, and pay them to the full.

Your hour when you may obtain from Me easily the pardon of all your sins.

Your hour when you may help yourself at will from the treasury of My Heart; when you may supply abundantly all the needs of your soul. When its defilement may be cleansed, its dryness refreshed, its wounds healed, its resistance conquered, its coldness warmed, its waywardness controlled. I am your Guest. I have to compensate you for My entertainment. Ask what you will, this is your hour.

Your hour to bring to My feet all whom you love; all depending on you; all for whom you are anxious, with their miseries, and needs, and troubles. That they are yours will give them an additional claim on My Heart. Fear not to ask great things; to call on Me for extreme forbearance, for special interventions of mercy. The sense of your unworthiness, the consciousness of past sin may oppress you, the knowledge that I am Judge as well as Guest may tie your tongue. Fear not, My host, My kind entertainer—this is your hour. Do with Me what you will. Lead Me up and down among the rows of your sick. Bring to Me the blind, the halt, the leprous, the fever-stricken, and I will heal them.

It is your hour, to obtain for them all that your heart desires. Speak to Me for them now and I will listen; ask for them now and I will grant. Delight in your Lord while He is with you, and He will give you the desires of your heart. For every one that askrth now receiveth. Ask; seek; knock—for this is your hour.

Oblation and Petition, p. 10.

Prayer before a Crucifix, p. 12.

THE WELCOME OF A HOST

III

The Eighth day after the Resurrection.

Before Communion

SEE St. Thomas sitting apart from the rest in the Supper Room, cut off from them in all but bodily presence, sharing neither their joy, their enthusiasm, their brotherly intercourse, nor the strength that union by charity gives. Accounting himself strong-minded, he is obstinate, sullen, testy, gloomy, weak. He is drifting away from the Master for whom he has left all things, who has been to him all in all. What makes the difference between him and the others? The Presence of Christ. They are risen with Christ. Their joy, their hope, their very life that was buried with Him has revived with the Resurrection. To them their Master is not a glorious memory of the past, all the more bitter because of the expectation that had been raised. He is living, loving, and may be looked for in His glorious beauty at any moment.

He comes! He stands among them in the Supper Room, in His old place, the place always left for Him now. See how every eye turns instinctively to Thomas. For the eyes of his Master are turned to him. It is for him He has come tonight. Mark the instantaneous change wrought by that Presence, by that look. See Thomas as he hastens forward, his steps trembling with eagerness, his face aglow with love and with shame. See him as he falls at the pierced feet. Note the intensity of feeling in the clasped hands, the upturned face, the cry of joy: "My Lord and my God!"

O dearest Lord Jesus, I thank Thee with all my heart for having come to the rescue of that poor suffering Apostle, for having kept for Thyself and for Thy service that slow, yet loyal and generous soul. I adore Thee with his delight, his contrition, his whole-hearted oblation of himself into Thy hands. With him I welcome Thee today, and confess Thee, hidden beneath the sacramental veils, my Lord and my God.

My Lord—Man as one of us, Saviour, Head of our race, King of kings and Lord of lords, to whom is due my service, all that is mine, myself; to whom I give myself with the most absolute self-surrender, desiring only that Thou wouldst claim me, receive me, dispose of me as Thine in time and in eternity:

And my God—very God of very God, consubstantial with the Father: by whom all things were made. Who for us men and for our salvation came down from heaven, and was made man:

My God—with whom I have relations intimate and tender beyond my power to conceive. My First Beginning, my Last End, whom I must reach and secure as my own possession in eternity, or be forever miserable:

My Lord and my God—uniting in Thyself every claim to my loyalty, my worship, my tenderest love. Oh make Thyself more and more to my soul! I believe in Thee here truly present, but increase my faith. I hope in Thee, yet not as Thy goodness deserves. I love Thee, but not as I desire. Let Thy Blessed Presence in frequent Communion do gradually for me what in an instant it did for Thomas. Let it come to influence my every thought, and word, and act. Wake up in my soul all that can glorify Thee, that with all Thou hast given me I may make Thee a return of love, and content myself in contenting Thee, my Lord and my God!

After Communion

"My Lord and my God!"

"Lord, I believe; help Thou my unbelief."

"Thou art Christ, the Son of the living God."

"O Lord my God, I will give praise to Thee for ever and ever" (Ps. 29:13).

"Whence is this to me that my Lord should come to me?"

"Lord, I am not worthy that Thou should come under my roof."

"O my soul, bless the Lord, and let all that is within me bless His holy Name" (Ps. 102:1).

"Bless the Lord, O my soul, and never forget all He hath done for thee" (*Ibid.*).

"Bless the Lord, all ye servants of the Lord, who stand in the house of the Lord, in the courts of the house of our God" (Ps. 133:1).

"O magnify the Lord with me, and let us extol His Name together" (Ps. 33:4).

"For this is God, our God unto eternity, and for ever and ever" (Ps. 47:15).

"Oh, how hast Thou magnified Thy mercy, O God" (Ps. 35:8).

"Let them say so that have been redeemed by the Lord, whom He hath redeemed from the hand of the enemy" (Ps. 106:2).

"Thou art worthy, O Lord our God, to receive glory, and honour, and power" (Apoc. 4:11).

"Amen. Benediction, and glory, and thanksgiving, honour, and power, and strength to our God for ever and ever. Amen" (Apoc. 7:12).

My God, I adore thee. Adoration is as yet little more to me than a name. When I see Thee as Thou art, I shall marvel at the condescension that makes Thee accept my adoration now.

And I shall marvel no less at the cold thanksgivings of earth. Oh, with what vehemence will my soul pour itself forth when the restraints of this life are no more! Like a mighty flood long pent up, that breaks at length through dam and dyke and laps the city on every side, will be my thanksgiving in Heaven. So will it leap up for ever in Thy Presence, fresh and free, magnifying the Lord, striving with all the energy of its being to render Him something like a return for all He has rendered unto me.

Wait, my God, wait a little while for that hour. All hours are before Thee now. Already Thou seest me in my place before Thy throne. Already my glad praise goes up before Thee, and seeing it, Thou hast compassion on my feeble efforts now. Wait, wait a little while, and I will pay Thee all.

Meanwhile let me fall back on the treasures of others. Let me share in the adoration and thanksgiving with which Thomas welcomed Thee on the octave day of the Resurrection. Thou wert his Guest in the Supper Room. It was for him that Thou didst come. The happiness of that sweet evening the rest owed to him. As Thy host, he came forward in trembling joy to do Thee reverence, to make reparation for that slowness of belief which was Thy one reproach to the Eleven, to acknowledge by his glorious confession the union in Thy Sacred Person of the Divine and Human Natures.

With him I cry to Thee here truly present: "My Lord and my God!" Happier than he, I take from Thy lips the blessing of those who have not seen and have believed.

Teach me, dear Lord, my duties as a host. Let me learn them from Martha and from Thomas. A host lays himself out to entertain his guest. He forgets His own likes and dislikes to consult the tastes of the friend whose comfort and happiness depend on the thoughtful kindness and genuine welcome accorded him.

Lord, Thou art with me now. I know not how to entertain so great a Majesty, but at least let me not transgress the laws of human courtesy. Let me offer Thee the hospitality of eastern lands and of olden times, the humble services, the kindliness that welcomes the coming and speeds the parting guest. I must not leave Thee alone during the brief moments of Thy stay. I must set aside all other claims and cares and keep myself free for attendance on Thee, for converse with Thee. And this converse will be about things that interest Thee, concerns that I know Thou hast at heart. The names of those near and dear to Thee will come in. I shall make my own the burdens and the sufferings of Thy friends, and offer myself for any service that affection for them for Thy sake may prompt. I shall sorrow with Thee, Lord, in Thy sorrows, enter into Thy designs, be concerned when Thy glory is imperilled, bring eager reparation for Thy wrongs. "Whatever touches the Church and souls redeemed with Thy Precious Blood, whatever calls for prayer, will be matter of earnest converse with Thee during the brief moments of Thy stay.

Thy beloved Disciple tells us, Lord, that Thou wouldst not trust Thyself to any man, for Thou knewest what was in man. How is it, then, that Thou dost trust Thyself to me? Is it because I am to be depended on;

that I value so truly the treasure I have in the Eucharist; that I shall turn it to such good account—is it so, O Lord? Alas! it is because Thou knowest me so well, that Thou shouldst refrain from trusting Thyself to me. Thou needest no one to tell Thee what Thou must expect if Thou wilt make Thyself my Guest. And in spite of all, Thou hast come.

I cannot offer Thee much, O Lord, at Thy coming, but I can bid Thee welcome. I can embrace Thee and hold Thee fast. I kiss Thy feet, O my Master, I kiss Thy feet. With nothing in my hand to offer Thee, with none of the generosity and zeal in Thy service that others bring, I have yet the humble welcome which not all my shortcomings can check. This will suffice me. As Thou crossest the threshold at the end of Thy visit, I shall be content if Thou canst say to Thy Angels: "She hath not ceased to kiss My feet."

Oblation and Petition, p. 82.

Prayer before a Crucifix, p. 12.

LA JOURNÉE d'Hier

DIEU SEUL

HIER

LA JOURNÉE d'Aujourd'hui

TRAVAILLER

AIMER

SOUFFRIR

AUJOURD'HUI

PRIER et ESPÉRER

THE WELCOME
OF A TOILER

THE WELCOME OF A TOILER

I

"Ordering all things sweetly"—Wisdom 8:1.

Before Communion

HOW sweetly has the life of the Son of God on earth been ordered with a view to our salvation and our help! Had we been asked whether a commonplace, uneventful life, or one of marvels and miracles would best achieve the end for which Messiah came, we should have been at a loss how to reply. Manifestations of Divine power would accredit His mission, but they would make His life one for our admiration rather than for our imitation. On the other hand, a lowly position and an ordinary career would want the prestige belonging to the Redeemer and universal Teacher of mankind. How could both needs be met? How should He be at once the

Wonder-worker to sustain our faith and our hope, and our Companion in the un-heroic paths of daily life?

We could never have guessed. We might have imagined the stilling of the tempest, the healing of every disease and every infirmity. But we could no more have suspected the thirty years of toil in the workshop of Nazareth, than we could have reconciled the Transfiguration on Thabor with the scene beneath the olive trees, or the three hours on Calvary. Yet all has been harmonised for the confirmation of our faith and hope, and for the sustaining of our courage along the toilsome way of homely duty by the force of His example who is like to us in all things, save only sin. Thabor, Gethsemane, Calvary, are our resource in the crucial hours of life, in the strife between the spirit and the flesh, which reduces to an agony. But these seasons are the exception, and the lessons they call for were briefly given. A few moments He showed Himself to us as our glorified Head; a few hours as our Model in the extremity of mental and physical pain. But for the monotonous round of labour which is the rule of our life, He judged a corresponding term of teaching to be necessary. And so we have the thirty years of hidden life in the cottage and the workshop of Nazareth.

It is only because we have not studied it in detail that this period of Our Lord's life appears less wonderful than the years of miracles or the death of the Cross. In one sense it is more wonderful. That earth, and sea, and disease, and death should obey Him, that all nature should be convulsed on Calvary, is not surprising. But that God could do anything commonplace, that He should be a helpless Babe, an errand Boy, a tradesman—His back bowed beneath burdens, His hands hardened with toil, His work of the simplest and commonest, uninteresting, unnoticed, bringing Him no reputation—could it have entered into the heart of man to conceive this?

Nazareth is the school in which all must learn. In whatever station of life our lot may be cast, there must be labour, and labour sanctified. Though heaven has been opened to us by the death on the Cross, it has still to be earned as a reward. It is set before us as a kingdom to be won by violence, as a treasure revealed to earnest search. Work of mind or body is the price all must pay for eternal rest. We must bring to God His gifts improved by industry if we are to be welcomed as faithful servants; we must work in the vineyard if we are to expect the hire when evening comes.

Many of us look upon labour as a hard necessity. Yet it was a law in Eden itself before it became a punishment: "The Lord God took man, and put him into the paradise of pleasure to dress it and to keep it." And when sin brought the decree: "In the sweat of thy brow thou shalt eat bread," labour was to be no mere penalty, even then, but a remedy and a safeguard. It is to heal what sin has wounded, to ward off the moral evils that rush in upon the indolent soul, as the sea upon low-lying lands when the dykes are swept away.

We know this, we feel it by the intimate conviction of experience, and nevertheless we are not reconciled to our lot. Our courage flags under the burden and heat of the day. There are times when the monotony of life chafes the most enduring of us. Therefore our Head would bear it first. Toil should have the unspeakable honour of being consecrated by the touch of His hands. It should be made easy to us by the example of the Man God, poor and in labours from His youth. In a little bit of a village hidden amid the hills; among country folk, uncouth and of ill-repute; in a two-roomed house, and a workshop up the street, He would spend the greater part of His life on earth.

See it—a wooden shed wedged in between two others—the workshop of the Son of God. Let us creep in, and kneel down, and watch. He has laid aside his upper garment to allow his limbs free play. His face, and neck, and arms are bronzed by exposure, for half

His work is done out of doors, in the small enclosure yonder where you see the logs. The veins stand out in the delicate, sensitive hands, the palms are hard with toil. He uses now the saw, now the plane, now the hammer, as He makes and mends cart-wheels, tables, stools, all the furniture of that rude, out-of-the-way place. His work is well done, but it is rough. His tools are clumsy. Everything in the shape of carpentering is in a very backward state here at Nazareth. He gets no thanks for His work. No store is set by it. No one knows it or prizes it as His. There is no keeping of relics. When it is done with, it will be thrown aside or burnt like anything else. So far from gaining any reputation by those long years of labour, they rather stood in His way when His time for preaching came: "Is not this the carpenter?" Can anything good come from Nazareth?

He works alone. He could not pay an assistant. The division of labour which goes so far to lessen its difficulties and its irksomeness, is not for Him. Now and again He pauses through sheer exhaustion, and wipes His heated brow. The sun mounts high in the heavens, the sun of that sultry land; but He is a poor man and must work on, work against time. Now He lifts His head, a villager has come in, and He goes forward to receive orders. At noon there is a short respite, and the thought of Mary, and the heart to heart converse with her during their simple meal and prayer together, brings Him refreshment and gladness. But the afternoon sees Him hard at work again. What He has made and mended has to be carried on His shoulders to the little homes about. He waits while it is examined and criticised. However low He has priced His labour, He is beaten down as a matter of course. He holds out His hand for His pay, and thanks His employer, and goes back to His shop to sweep up the shavings and leave all neat and ready for the morrow.

And this day after day, year after year. Always the same round of humble duties—making, mending, journeying to and fro; His tasks set by others, and subject to their criticism and caprice. No beholder to note the perfection of every act, of every movement: to see the uplifted eye; to hear the whispered prayer; to be helped by His patience and His perseverance; to share His pain at rebuffs, and unkindness, and blame undeserved.

O wonderful mystery of that hidden life of daily toil, how ill could we have spared it from the three-and-thirty years! Hither we come for rest and for strength, for example and consolation, all our lives through. Well did Thy wisdom and Thy love counsel

Thee, Lord, to give to this task of silent teaching the longest part of Thy earthly life. A month, a week of such teaching would have been an unutterable condescension and help. But it would not have had the force given by the perseverance of years. It is not the difficulty of any work at the outset that we feel. Hand and brain will give themselves eagerly to labour when the charm of novelty is upon it. Difficulties do but add zest to our exertions—at the start. But when monotony begins to tire, when we see nothing before us, perhaps through long years, but the dreary vista of the same humdrum toil, it is then that we need the workshop of Nazareth; it is then that we understand the invitation: "Come to Me, all you who labour."

There was no excitement in the little home at Nazareth. No elegant artistic articles drew the eyes of men to the Carpenter's shop. He was no distinguished man among His fellows, that village tradesman. Yet the world lay in the hollow of His hand, and the mightiest works of human genius to His infinite wisdom had been sport. To teach us patience and obedience, and the secret of real greatness in the obscurity of a humble home, Jesus of Nazareth toiled amid dust and shavings for the better part of twenty years. Thither He calls all those whose lot on earth is like His own. He calls them in these restless, feverish days to look and ponder, to unlearn the world's judgments and learn of Him. He holds out His reward: "Learn of Me that I am meek and humble of heart, and you shall find rest to your souls."

Call me, O Lord, and bid me come to Thee. Let me watch Thee in Thy poor home and at Thy lowly trade. Keep me by Thy side till the lessons of Thy life and the dispositions of Thy Heart have passed into mine. Let me see Thy form, bowed beneath the burdens carried to and fro; Thy hands laid to the drudgery of the saw, the hammer, the broom; Thy mind given to the petty details of the village carpentry. And seeing this, can I, O Master, go on reckoning by the world's standards? Can I repine at my station or my means, and harbour thoughts of impatience or regret? Shall I not rather account myself blessed if I am called to share, in any degree, Thy lot?

Let me not be among the restless and the self-seeking who want vocations that are no call of Thine; who fret because Thy service means doing Thy Will and not their own; who keep their gaiety and their attractiveness for strangers, and their discourtesy and moroseness for their own homes. Lord, let me realise that I belong not to myself but to Thee, that I came into this world, not as a proprietor into his domain, but as a servant to watch and wait for his master's beck.

And make me feel that that beck is a call to happiness no less than to service, happiness inseparable from faithful service, happiness begun here, to be perfected in the life to come.

Why should I seek to carve out a path for myself when there is one of Thy choosing at my door? Why not loyally accept Thy Will for me in events and circumstances, instead of rebelling against them or trying to modify them after an ideal of my own? Had the marble of Michelangelo been capable of a wish, it would have been simply this—that there might be nothing in it to mar the great master's work, that it might so yield itself to his hand as to bring out his conception fully. Let me enter into Thy designs for myself and others, not with the passiveness of unresisting matter, but with the zeal of a servant devoted to the interests of his master, the loving eagerness of a friend to fall in with the plans of a friend. Thou art more to me, infinitely more, than master or friend. All devotedness and eager love are called for when there is question of co-operating with Thee. As far as I can understand Thy action in all that happens, it shall call forth my praise. When Thy "ways are past finding out," I will adore them in silence and in trust.

Jesus, who in Thy days of humble toil pleased God, who couldst say: "I do always the things that please Him" (John 8:29), come to me today to make my heart like Thine. Unite me so closely to Thyself that I too, in every thought, and word, and deed, may be acceptable to God, and do always the things that please Him.

AFTER COMMUNION

"Holy, Holy, Holy, Lord God of hosts!"

"Thou art Christ, the Son of the Living God."

"My Lord and my God."

"Truly Thou art a hidden God" (Isa. 45:15).

"O Lord, how great are Thy works! Thy thoughts are exceeding deep" (Ps. 91:6).

"Give praise to our God, all ye His servants: and you that fear Him, little and great" (Apoc. 19:5).

"Thou art worthy, O Lord our God, to receive glory, and honour, and power" (Apoc. 4:11).

And therefore with Angels and Archangels, with Thrones and Dominations, and with all the heavenly army, we sing a hymn to Thy glory, saying: "Holy, Holy, Holy, Lord God of hosts. Heaven and earth are full of Thy glory. Hosanna in the highest. Blessed is He that cometh in the Name of the Lord. Hosanna in the highest."

"Master, where dwellest Thou?"

"Come and see."

"Can anything of good come from Nazareth?"

"Come and see."

Yes, dearest Lord, all good has come to us thence, for Thou, Jesus of Nazareth, art all our good. All divine lessons, all the force of a divine example, all help, and strength, and consolation for our humdrum work has come to us from that little bit of a shop at the bottom of the village street. This was Thy recompense. This was the joy set before Thee for the sake of which Thou didst cheerfully endure the monotony and hardship of those weary years. We think of Thee as lonely in that obscure spot, almost as wasting there an example that would have revolutionised the world had it been shown under other conditions of time and place. But Thy wisdom was reaching from end to end mightily, and ordering all things sweetly. All time was before Thee; and thronging round Thee, adoring, thanking, drinking in Thy teaching, were all who in every age would come hither to learn. Not Saints alone, but each one of us, however lowly, was present to Thee there. Each one can say: "He loved me and delivered Himself for me" to that life of toil and trouble. He knows what it is to have to work on when brain and arm are weary, when nature cries out for break or change in the task to which we rise each morning.

Shall not Thy example, O loving Lord, be my strength, and Thy sympathy my all-sufficient consolation? I have to show my gratitude to Thee.

I have to make a personal return for what was done as much for me as if it had been for me alone. How shall I do this except by proving that Thou hast not laboured for me in vain?

Teach me, my God, the lesson of Nazareth. Give me to see the law of labour in its true light, to accept it in any shape in which Thy Providence may lay it at my door. And if I find it not there, to go forth and seek it as the material of which my happiness here and hereafter must be fashioned, as my safeguard, my title to reward. Let me love it still more because it likens me to Thee.

And let my work be worthy of the name. Not one of the many devices for killing time. Not taken up on the whim of the moment and cast aside as soon as it proves laborious or irksome. But occupation that taxes the energy of limb, and brain, and soul; that entails application and fatigue; that calls for the sacrifice of leisure and natural inclination. Let it be done and faithfully done, not because I am obliged, not because it is remunerative or interesting, but because it is the expression of my love, because it is my service of Thee.

At Nazareth Thou hast taught us the worth of little things done for God. But how slow we are to learn our lesson! Unless we can make a show, we suppose we are doing nothing. If anything will teach me the value of humble, unobtrusive toil, surely it is the workshop there. And it will teach me if I look long and quietly, and try to do my work at my Master's side, watching Him, noting how He works, observing His eyes, and lips, and hands, looking into His Heart.

And since my work is poor and worthless and unworthy of Thy acceptance, unite it, Lord, with Thine, and offer it with the merit of Thine infinitely precious labours to the Father for me. Daily in the Mass those merits are made over to me. I desire to appropriate them, and through Thy hands to offer all I have and am to God. *"Per Ipsum, et cum Ipso, et in Ipso,"* by Thee, with Thee, in Thee, may all I do, and say, and suffer be presented to the Father and be made pleasing in Thy sight.

O Jesus of Nazareth, bring home to all the toilers of earth the lessons of Thy holy hidden life. Show all men how labour has been ennobled, sweetened, and sanctified by Thee; how all our work by union with Thine may become precious in the sight of God, and purchase for us eternal rest and joy when evening comes and the labourers receive their hire.

Oblation and Petition, p. 82.
Prayer before a Crucifix, p. 12.

THE WELCOME OF A TOILER

II

"Man is born to labour"—Job 5:7.

THE LAW of labour is upon us all. Head or hand, or both, must carry out the sentence pronounced in Paradise on every child of Adam. But besides the bodily toil to which we rise each morning, there is another more important and more onerous, from which none is exempt. St. Paul puts it before us with his usual energy of expression when writing to his converts at Philippi he says: "Work out your salvation with fear and trembling" (Philip 2:12). And again in the comprehensive phrase: "Put on Christ" (Galat. 3:27).

To work a thing out implies strenuous effort and patient perseverance. A problem is not worked out when we leave its solution to chance, or trust to its coming right of itself. All work that is to be a success must have devoted to it intelligent and persistent labour, and a will prepared to surmount all difficulties. No building is raised, no art acquired, no victory gained on other conditions. And the "one thing necessary" is not to be secured at a less price. We are sent into the world for the one purpose of bringing ourselves into conformity with our Head, that we may be worthy to share His glory. "For whom He foreknew, He also predestinated to be made conformable to the image of His Son" (Rom. 8:29).

To the Ephesians St. Paul speaks of "learning Christ" (Ephes. 4:20). It is a difficult task, but the toil is divided between Master and pupils. A good teacher prepares long and carefully. He counts no pains too great, no instruments too costly, no details too small to deserve attention. His part done, it remains for the learners to do theirs. They must bring to their lesson a docile, eager, receptive mind, an attentive eye and ear, a resolute will, if there is to be any satisfactory result. If interest flags, the best lesson will fall flat, and—who shall tell with what disappointment to the teacher?

Dear Master, how long and how painfully hast Thou prepared Thy lessons for me! Far back in the Eternal years were Bethlehem, and Nazareth, Gethsemane, and Calvary decreed, and their every circumstance fitted to my need. An Angel teacher might have been assigned me, and surely this had been an inestimable grace. But the Lord of Angels would have no substitute. He must come Himself. By His own lips were the hard truths to be taught. By His own practice should they be softened. By His own grace should they bear fruit.

St. Paul calls attention to the marvellous love of God in condescending to become Himself our Teacher. "The goodness and kindness of God our Saviour hath appeared to all men, instructing us . . ." (Titus 3:4). And shall I not be grateful! And shall I not care to learn! And when kings and prophets have desired to see and hear what is granted to me, shall I be heedless and indifferent!

We have to "put on Christ." It is a consequence of our baptism, St. Paul tells us (Galat. 3:27). But what a transformation the words suggest; what a putting aside of things that cling to us as part of our very selves, before we can be "clothed upon;" before we can put on Christ! Lord, what a change must come about in my soul before I am in any respect like Thee! What a contrast is there between Thy love and joyous acceptance of the Father's Will, and my mistrust and frequent rejection of that blessed Will to follow the perversity of my own! Between Thy holiness and my sinfulness—Between Thy fortitude through a life of suffering, and my impatience under the least annoyance—Between the sublime self-immolation of thy life, and the utter selfishness of mine. Lord, where shall I begin: have I as yet begun my life's work of learning Thee?

"Learn of Me that I am meek and humble of heart."

Thou hast Thyself marked out my course—where I am to begin and—where I am to end. For if I am like Thee in Thy meekness and humility, I shall be like Thee wholly; I shall have put on Christ.

Lord, help me! For it is just in these two points that I am most unlike Thee. I look at Thy self-forgetfulness, Thy gentle, courteous ways; Thy compassion for the poor and suffering; Thy tender sympathy for all in need; Thy lowliness of heart and readiness for humble service; and in the midst of unparalleled insult and injury, Thy serenity and peace of heart.

And my heart! Its hardness and its selfishness; my unkind thoughts and criticism; my harsh tones; my exacting ways; my stinginess in giving time and interest and sympathy; my slowness in acts of charity that cost! There is self-seeking in all my dealings with others; even in my dealings with Thee. If I neglect prayer;

if I play with temptation; if I fail in the duties of my state—self-indulgence is at the root of all.

What shall I do, Lord? What remedy can put right so much that is wrong?

"Fear not; behold your God" (Isa. 40:9).

"Fear not and be not dismayed: for the Lord will be with thee and will not leave thee nor forsake thee, till thou hast finished all the work for the service" (1 Par. 28:20).

Help me then, dear Lord. This shall be my encouragement in the struggle with self, that I fight not alone or on my own account, but "for the service." The cause is Thine, my King, and Thou art ever at hand with all needful grace. By the kindness of Thy looks, and words, and listening, give me kind looks and words for all. Make me like Thee in my dealings with others, especially with the companions of my daily life. Show me where selfishness hides, and help me to overcome a little every day. Teach me to accommodate myself to those of a different character from my own; to make allowances for mistakes and misunderstanding, for the pressure of trial or of work. Let my first instinct be that of Thy Blessed Mother at Cana—not to censure, but to pity, to excuse, to help. Let me deserve mercy by being always merciful.

Victory over self can be won only by frequent and earnest effort. And effort will cost. But I can do all things in Him who strengthens me, who comes to me today to pour into my heart the treasures of His.

"Strengthen me, O Lord God" (Judith 13:7).

"Give me constancy in my mind . . . and fortitude, that I may overthrow my enemies" (Judith 9:14).

"Strengthen me that I may bring to pass that which I have purposed, having a belief that it might be done by Thee" (Judith 13:7).

AFTER COMMUNION

"Fear not; behold your God" (Isa. 40:9).

"It is I, be not afraid" (John 6:20).

"Holy, Holy, Holy, Lord God of hosts."

"Let all the earth adore Thee and sing to Thee" (Ps. 65:4).

"Let all Thy Angels and Saints bless Thee, and praise Thee, and glorify Thee for ever" (Dan. 3:58).

"Give praise to our God, all ye His servants: and you that fear Him, little and great" (Apoc. 19:5).

"O bless our God, and make the voice of His praise to be heard" (Ps. 65:8).

"For who is God but the Lord, or who is God but our God?" (Ps. 17:32).

"Thou art worthy, O Lord our God, to receive glory, and honour, and power: because Thou hast created all things, and for Thy will they were, and have been created" (Apoc. 4:11).

"The Lord is with thee." How often are these words upon my lips! How often do I congratulate the Blessed among women on this her supreme, happiness: *"Ave, gratia plena, Dominus tecum!"* And behold! at this moment as I kneel bowed down, my hands folded upon my breast, congratulations—could I only hear them—are around me on every side.

"The Lord is with thee" my Good Angel is saying, as he makes his thanksgiving beside me, adoring, praising, loving Him whom he beholds beneath the veils. "O child, rejoice and give thanks, 'for this is God, our God unto eternity, and for ever and ever' (Ps. 47:15). Having Him thou hast all things. All that is due to Him is now in thy power to give. All thy need He is here to satisfy. 'O magnify the Lord with me, and let us extol His name together'" (Ps. 33:4).

"The Lord is with thee," say the Blessed, remembering their own Communions, enjoying now the fruits of their faith, seeing how their Communions on earth were the principle of all the grace that has now blossomed into glory; the principle, too, of the glorious resurrection awaiting the body when its hour shall come. "The Lord is with thee! The Lord is with thee!" they say

to me. Oh, profit by His Presence, every instant of which is rich in eternal fruit.

"The Lord is with thee!" say the holy waiting Souls, in wistful supplication. "He is with thee who is so easily appeased on earth, the realm of mercy; whose judgments are so rigorous when life and time are past. Lift up for us the prayer He has come on purpose to hear. Stretch out to us the hands He is filling with gifts, that through your riches your poor brethren may go free."

"The Lord is with thee" the Holy Trinity Itself says to me. "More than this Gift God Himself cannot give thee; less would not meet thy wants. Pressing upon thee at all times are thy duties as a creature—adoration, thanksgiving, praise; of a sinful and needy creature—prayer for mercy, and for all things necessary for soul and body. The Lord is with thee now to pay all thy debts; to adore, and praise, and give thanks in thy name; to forgive all thy sins; to supply all thy need. How hath He not with Himself given thee all things?

"Thou art weak and unstable. The devil and the world are strong. But I am the most mighty God, fear not."

"A treacherous and more dangerous foe assails thee from within. Restless passions continually disturb thy peace and threaten thee with destruction. 'Fear not, nor be afraid of them' (Deut. 1:29). 'If thou say in thy heart: These enemies are more than I, how shall I be able to destroy them? Fear not, because the Lord thy God is in the midst of thee. He will consume them by little and little and by degrees; thou wilt not be able to destroy them altogether lest thou shouldst say in thy heart: My own might and the strength of my own hand have achieved all these things for me, and thy heart be lifted up. But the Lord thy God shall slay them until they be utterly destroyed' (Deut. 7:17). 'He shall cast out the enemy from before thee, and shall say: Be thou brought to nought' (Deut. 33:27). 'Let not your heart, then, be dismayed; be not afraid; fear them not; because the Lord your God is in the midst of you, and will fight for you against your enemies, to deliver you from danger' (Deut. 20:3).

"Thou art sick, sick even unto death? I am come to heal thee. 'They that are whole need not the Physician, but they that are sick' (Luke 5:31). 'The Lord will take away from thee all sickness, and the grievous infirmities which thou knowest' (Deut. 7:15).

"Thou art 'wretched and miserable, and poor, and blind, and naked.' With a wistful eye thou beholdest the riches of others—the generosity and self-sacrifice, the humility and patience, the charity, faith, fortitude of the Saints? Be of good courage. 'Are not these things stored up with Me?' (Deut. 32:34). Have I not with Myself given thee all things?

"Friends fall away with years, and a sense of solitude weighs upon thee more and more? 'Behold I am with thee all days' (Matt, 28:20), 'the Faithful and True' (Apoc. 19:11). 'God is not as a man that He should lie, nor as the son of man that He should be changed' (Numb, 23:19). 'I am the Lord, and I change not' (Malach. 3:6). 'I have loved thee with an everlasting love' (Jer. 31:3). 'I have called thee by thy name, thou art Mine' (Isa. 45:4).

"Life is long, and the way is dreary, and thou art bowed down beneath the burden of the day and the heats. 'Do manfully, and let thy heart take courage' (Ps. 26:14). 'Wait on God with patience, join thyself to God, and endure' (Ecclus. 2:3). 'For behold short years pass away, and thou art walking in a path by which thou shalt not return'" (Job 16:23).

"O God, my strong One, in Thee will I trust: my rock, and my strength, and my Saviour" (2 Kings 22:3). "For there is no other God but Thou, who hast care of all. And because Thou art Lord of all, Thou makest Thyself gracious to all" (Wisd. 12:13). "Grant me this grace, that with all my strength I may love Him that made me" (Ecclus. 7:32), "and fear Thee and serve Thee with my whole heart" (1 Kings 12:27). "To the work of Thy hands reach out Thy right hand" (Job 14:15). "And let me cleave to Thee, O Lord, my God."

Lord Jesus, I do indeed desire to be conformed to Thee, my Head. I desire to be like Thee here that I may be like Thee and with Thee hereafter. I know that a member, daintily treated, ill becomes a Head that has suffered so much. I know, too, that though Thy coming to me in Holy Communion is to make me like Thyself, the change will be a gradual one, brought about by my own efforts, helped by Thy grace. It will not be sudden; it will not be painless. Only by means of repeated acts can I put off myself and put on Christ. I must not avoid, but use well the opportunities Thy Providence will place in my way. There will be many failures. But I will not be discouraged. "God is my strong One, in Him will I trust" (2 Kings 22:3). The work is His, He will accomplish it in His own time. Quietly and gradually He will transform me into His likeness, that I may be able to say in my measure: "I live, now not I, but Christ liveth in me" (Galat. 2:20).

Oblation and Petition, p. 82.

Prayer before a Crucifix, p. 12.

THE WELCOME
OF A SUPPLIANT

THE WELCOME OF A SUPPLIANT

I

"Lord, help me!"

BEFORE COMMUNION

"AND He went Into the coasts of Tyre and Sidon; and entering into a house He would that no man should know it, and He could not be hid. For a woman of Canaan, as soon as she heard of Him, came in and fell down at His feet, and crying out said to Him: Have mercy on me, O Lord, Thou Son of David, my daughter is grievously troubled by a devil."

She was one of those who will dare anything, brave everything, to gain the desire of their heart. She had heard of the Wonder-worker who was going through the length and breadth of His own land doing good to all, and healing every disease and every infirmity among the people. Oh that He would come her way!

She was not one of His; but once within reach of her prayer He should not depart till He had heard and answered it.

One day she was startled by the tidings that He had crossed the borders of Judea, and was in the coasts of Tyre and Sidon. Instantly her resolution was taken. She would find Him. She would throw herself at His feet. Her poor child should be cured at last. Nothing stayed her; neither fear of rebuff, nor the warning that He would have no one know where He was, nor the fear of angering Him by the intrusion of a Gentile.

She came in and fell down at His feet: "Have mercy on me, O Lord, Thou Son of David, my daughter is grievously troubled by a devil."

Who answered her not a word.

What a reception! And she had heard He was so tender, and so merciful, that He listened to all, heard the prayers of all. But she would take no refusal. He must, He *must* take pity on her child. She crouched low at His feet. Now it is a sob, now a passionate cry:

"Have mercy on me, have mercy on me, O Son of David!"

She is making herself a nuisance. The Twelve gathered round our Lord turn angrily upon her and bid her stop. Their Master does not mean to do anything for the pagan people of this land; she must be quiet and go home. As if she had not heard them, she continues her pitiful cry:

"Have mercy on me."

They turn to our Lord and beseech Him saying: "Send her away, for she crieth after us."

And He takes their part: "I was not sent but to the sheep that are lost of the house of Israel."

"Lord, help me," is her only reply. No sign of discouragement, of having taken amiss what seemed so hard; only that earnest, trusting cry: "Lord, help me!"

Our Lord looks down upon her. He sees the agony of her soul. Her prayer is perfect. She has done all she can. And still He does not relent. Nay, His words grow sterner as the fervour of her prayer grows more intense.

"It is not good to take the bread of the children and to cast it to the dogs."

How can He speak like this? Has she come so far to be called a dog? See how splendidly she bears the rebuff. She is not piqued. Her humble trust does not give way. Like Jacob she is strong against God. acob wrestled with an angel; she measures her strength with the Lord of Angels, with God Himself. See the ingenuity with which she turns His words to her own purpose; "Yea, Lord, for the whelps also eat under the table, of the crumbs of the children. I do not ask for the bread, but only for the crumbs that fall, the crumbs the children will not miss."

Our Lord is conquered. "O woman, great is thy faith; be it done to thee as thou wilt." And her daughter was cured from that hour.

Was it worth while to have waited, and trusted, and wrestled in prayer so long? Was it reward enough to look up to Him and see His smile, and hear from His lips that glorious praise? He who felt so keenly the want of faith in His chosen people, who again and again had rebuked His own disciples for their little faith, had found what He sought in this poor sheep outside the fold of Israel. And His delighted admiration broke forth in words that must have startled the Twelve: "O woman, great is thy faith; be it done to thee as thou wilt."

Only a woman could have shown such tact, have dared to make capital out of such a rebuff. And perhaps we may add—only a woman would He have tried so sorely. He who knows what is in man feared not to test to the utmost her faith and her forbearance. He knows that a woman's heart will brook delay, contempt, reproach, in the pursuit of its end, and never desist till its cause is won.

We notice that her prayer gains in fervor and persistence from the severity and prolongation of her trial. And as it grows in intensity and perfection, she simply asks for help without naming her need. We may follow her example here, and put our trouble before the pitying Heart of Jesus without even asking for help—the help we know will come. So the sisters at Bethany did when their brother Lazarus lay dying: "Lord, he whom thou lovest is sick." Or we may tell our wants, and wait in patient trust for Him to provide. So she did, at whose prayer His first miracle was wrought at Cana of Galilee. "They have no wine." He will sooner anticipate His time, break through nature's laws, work any sign, than suffer to go unheeded a trustful prayer.

The Mother of Jesus taught us at Cana not to be disheartened by a rebuff. "Woman, what is it to Me and to thee? My hour is not yet come." They were stern words. Did she give up all for lost? Did she desist? She looked up into His face—the face she knew so well—and there was that in it which belied the severity of His speech. Turning to the waiters she said: "Whatsoever He shall say to you, do ye." His time was not yet come; but a trusting prayer has its way with Him at all times. She hoped in Him, and was not confounded.

And lest I should say that such privilege was for His Mother only, I have the example of the pagan woman whose sole plea lay in her need, her recourse to Him, her humility, her perseverance. To excuse, maybe, the churlishness of the disciples, St. Matthew and St. Mark emphasize the fact that this poor suppliant had no claim upon our Lord. She was "a woman of Canaan, who came out of those coasts, a Gentile, a Syrophenician born." If she was a lost sheep, our Lord himself reminded her that she was not one of the house of Israel to whom He was sent. She was no child of the household, but a dog. Could words have been more crushing? They had not the slightest effect upon her trust. She had come to Him in her dire need; she was not going to leave Him unheard. She was deaf to stern, hard words, both from the Master and His followers. But she was not blind. She had looked up into the face of Jesus, and through His eyes she had read His Heart. What if the tones of His voice were against her—there was sympathy there. She was not of His race, but He was of her nature. He was man; He was pitying:

"Son of David, have mercy on me!"

Son of David, have mercy on me! Thou art the same now, Lord, as the day that suffering mother knelt at Thy feet. My need today was present to Thee then. Thou didst try her faith so sorely, to strengthen mine.

Thou hast set this pagan woman as a model for the suppliants of all time. I will study her; I will learn of her. Like her I will bear rebuff, delay, the agony of suspense. Like her I will trust in Thy Heart, and trusting, persevere in prayer. Lord, help me; Son of David, have mercy on me!

AFTER COMMUNION

"Blessed be the Lord this day" (3 Kings 5:7).

"O my soul, bless the Lord, and let all that is within me bless His holy Name" (Ps. 102:1).

"Bless the Lord, O my soul, and never forget all He hath done for thee" (*Ibid.*).

"Bless the Lord, all you His Angels, you that are mighty in strength" (*Ibid.*).

"Give praise to our God, all ye His servants: and you that fear Him, little and great" (Apoc. 19:5).

"O magnify the Lord with me, and let us extol His Name together" (Ps. 33:4).

"O bless our God, and make the voice of His praise to be heard" (Ps. 65:8).

"Blessed be the Lord, for He hath shown His wonderful mercy to me" (Ps. 30:22).

"For He hath satisfied the empty soul, and hath filled the empty soul with good things" (Ps. 106:9).

"It is not meet to take the bread of the children and to cast it to the dogs."

"Yea, Lord, for the whelps also eat of the crumbs that fall from the table of their masters."

"It is not good to admit a sinner and an outcast to the privileges of the children of God."

Yea, Lord, for Thou hast come to call not the just, but sinners. Thou wert called the Friend of sinners. Thou didst run out to meet the prodigal, and didst make him welcome to all the good things of his father's house.

"It is not meet that the Will of the Creator should bend to the will of the creature."

Yea, Lord, Thou didst bless "Israel Thy beloved" for that he was strong against God. And through all time it hath seemed good unto Thee that we should wrestle with Thee in prayer and prevail.

Remember, O Lord, that Thou hast bid us ask, and seek, and knock.

Remember that it is to importunity, not to merit, that Thy favour is promised: "For everyone that asks, receives; and he that seeks, finds; and to him that knocks, it shall be opened."

Remember that if we, being evil, know how to give good gifts to our children, much more will our

Father who is in heaven give good things to them that ask Him.

Remember Thou hast said: "If you ask the Father anything in My name He will give it you. Hitherto you have not asked anything in My name. Ask, and you shall receive, that your joy may be full."

Behold, I ask, and seek, and knock. I cry to Thee day and night. Hear me and have pity on me, lest continually coming, I weary Thee.

Because I continue knocking, rise and give to me. If not because I am Thy friend, yet because of my importunity give me all I need.

I cry after Thee with the Syrophenician woman: "Have mercy on me, O Lord, Thou Son of David." With her I come and adore Thee, saying: "Lord, help me."

Say to me as to the blind men of Capharnaum: "Do you believe that I can do this unto you?" And with full faith I will answer with them: "Yea, Lord."

Say to me: "If Thou canst believe, all things are possible to him that believeth." And I will cry out with tears: "I do believe; Lord, help my unbelief."

Say to me as to the blind man of Jericho: "What wilt thou that I do to thee?"

Say to me as to the sorrowing mother of Naim: "Weep not."

Yet, lest my prayer be one of those to which Thou wilt make answer: "You know not what you ask," one that is not conducive to my real welfare, or to the good of those for whom I pray, one that will be heard by the grant of something better—I add with Thee in the Garden:

"Abba, Father, all things are possible to Thee, remove this chalice from me. But yet not my will, but Thine be done. My Father, if this chalice may not pass away but I must drink it, Thy Will be done."

Oblation and Petition, pp. 160, 162.

Prayer before a Crucifix, p. 12.

THE WELCOME OF A SUPPLIANT

II

"And when she came to the man of God, she caught hold of his feet, and Giezi came to remove her. And the man of God said: Let her alone, for her soul is in anguish, and the Lord hath hid it from me, and hath not told me"
—4 Kings 4:27.

BEFORE COMMUNION

STERN and rugged men they seem to us, those prophets of the Old Law. Yet, how tender is Elias here, in presence of a mother's sorrow. He almost seems to take it ill that God had not told him of her trouble. He will not have her disturbed when she casts herself at his feet. He hears through her passionate expostulation: "Did I not ask a son of my Lord? did I not say to thee: Do not deceive me?" He anticipates her prayer and provides at once for her consolation.

"Go," he says to his servant, "and lay my staff upon the face of the child." He yields to her waywardness. But the mother of the child said: "As the Lord liveth, and as thy soul liveth, I will not leave thee." He arose, therefore, and followed her, and himself raised her child to life.

Will "the God of much compassion" (Exod. 34:6), "the God of all comfort" (2 Cor. 1:3), be less tender than His servant? Can we count too much on the pitying Heart of Christ our Lord when we come to His feet in desolation and distress? With a true instinct the Sunamitess discards such consolation as the prophet's servant might have offered her, and betakes herself to "the man of God" in whom she recognises the power and mercy of God Himself. She came to the man of God to Mount Carmel. And when the man of God saw her coming, he said to Giezi, his servant: "Go to meet her, and say to her: Is all well with thee, and with thy husband, and with thy son? And she answered: Well." A figure of the soul that looks not to creatures for consolation and help, that stops not to discuss its trouble with them, but flies straight to the Creator.

There are wounds which the touch of man only chafes and inflames. We must commit them to the one tender handling that will soothe their pain, "pouring in oil and wine." "Send them away," said the Apostles of the tired, hungry multitude who had flocked after our Lord into the desert. "Send her away," of the poor mother who came crying after Him for her suffering child. This is often the best we can expect from creatures in our need. I will turn for comfort and for help to the Creator, to Him who has said: "Call upon Me in the day of trouble, and I will deliver thee" (Ps. 49:15). "Him that cometh to Me, I will not cast out" (John 6:37).

"Arise, why sleepest Thou, O Lord? Arise, and cast us not off to the end: why turnest Thou Thy face away and forgettest our trouble?" (Ps. 43:23).

"O God, who art mighty above all, hear the voice of them "that have no other hope, and deliver me from my fear" (Esther 14:19).

"Deliver us by Thy hand, and help us who have no other helper but Thee, O Lord, who hast the knowledge of all things" (*Ibid.*).

"Remember, O Lord, and show Thyself to me in the time of my tribulation" (*Ibid.*).

"Help us, O God, our Saviour, and for the glory of Thy Name, O Lord, deliver us" (Ps. 78:9).

"Arise, O Lord, and help us for Thy Name's sake" (Ps. 43:26).

"I have regarded My own holy Name....It is not

for your sake that I will do this, but for My holy Name's sake" (Ezech. 36:22).

Lord, say thus to me as to Thy people of old. I know too well that wert Thou to consider me alone, my prayer must go unheard for ever. But it is not for my sake but for Thy own that I entreat Thee to hear and answer me. Remember Thy promise: "Whatsoever you shall ask the Father in My Name, that will I do: that the Father may be glorified in the Son. If you shall ask Me anything in My Name, that will I do" (John 14:13). I would rather it were to glorify Thy great Name than to reward any merit of mine that Thou shouldst listen to me and help me. Not to us, O Lord, not to us, but to Thy Name give glory.

After Communion

"Whence is this to me that my Lord should come to me?"

"For this is God, our God unto eternity, and for ever and ever" (Ps. 47:15).

"Thou art Christ, the Son of the living God."

"My Lord and my God."

"Lord, I believe; help Thou my unbelief."

"Lord, increase my faith."

"My soul doth magnify the Lord, and my spirit hath rejoiced in God my Saviour."

"For He hath satisfied the empty soul, and hath filled the hungry soul with good things" (Ps. 106:9).

"Give praise to our God, all ye His servants: and you that fear Him, little and great" (Apoc. 19:5).

"Sing praises to our God, sing ye; sing praises to our King, sing ye" (Ps. 46:7).

"Thou art worthy, O Lord our God, to receive glory, and honour, and power" (Apoc. 4:11).

"Amen. Benediction, and glory, and thanksgiving, honour, and power, and strength to our God for ever and ever. Amen" (Apoc. 7:12).

> *"Is all well with thee, and with thy husband,*
> *and with thy son?"* (4 Kings 4:26).

Our Lord is like us in all things. In our visits we ask after the household of our host. So does He. His concern extends to all that touches us, all who are dear to us, all whose lives are bound up with our own, and whose happiness depends in great measure on the character of our daily intercourse with them in the close relations of home life.

"Is all well with them? If not, why not? Tell me all about it," He says. He will not be put off with the plea that He knows already, and better than we can tell Him. He saw into the sad hearts of the two disciples on the road to Emmaus, yet He would hear their trouble from themselves. "Knowest Thou not the things that have been done," they asked. Who said to them, "What things?" He likes the confidence that comes to Him for sympathy as well as for help, that leads Him hither and thither: "Lord, come and see." A friend must hear of hopes, and plans, and family annoyances. He must be told how a conversation went well, or a mistake did harm, how there is friction in such a direction, and in another every effort to meet a difficulty has proved useless.

A friend must be a good listener. No one can come near our Lord in this respect. Hour after hour we may talk to Him, returning again and again upon the same old story, and He is never tired.

"Yes," some of us are sure to object, "there is this advantage, but on the other hand He is always silent; never a word in answer, never a sign to show interest or sympathy. How can conversation be kept up under such conditions?"

This is a difficulty certainly, though there are plenty of us to speak for the silent Friend, and testify to the Voice heard unmistakably in the depth of the soul. Light, consolation, strength—this is His answer to patient, persevering prayer. We hear no sound; we miss the sweetness of human tones; but it is help we should seek in prayer—help that is promised to prayer, not satisfaction.

Suppose those who have a suit before the law courts today were told that the judge was ready to give them the benefit of his advice, and so to sum up the case as to ensure its success, on condition that they should lay the affair before him—would this proviso be found too hard?

If a crowd of beggars were allowed access to a rich man who desired to help them, but required as a condition that he should be told of their need, and be allowed to aid in his own way and at his own time— would this deter them from besieging the rich man's gate, and wearing the steps of his doors?

If in the things of this world union is strength; if co-operation is one of the most potent factors of commercial success, and the counsel of experts a boon to be utilised to the full, why should there be less eagerness to secure it for the business of eternity?

O children of this world, what a perpetual reproach you are to the children of light! With all our faith, with all our prudence, how blind and foolish we show ourselves when there is question of the things of eternity and of the soul! Of course we should like the present satisfaction of a comforting word from our Prince, our Judge, our Divine Friend in the Tabernacle.

But is it for us to lay down the terms on which His favour is to be won? Because there is difficulty in prayer—and that there is, no one who has practised it will deny—are we going to forego all its privileges?

> *Prayer was not meant for luxury,*
> *Or selfish pastime sweet;*
> *It is the prostrate creature's place,*
> *At the Creator's feet.*[1]

For most of us prayer is no luxury. If occasionally it is an easy duty, a relief, it is oftener weary labour, and at times a veritable agony. But what of that, if by this labour and through this agony we are earning the present help we need, and the free, blissful, face-to-face intercourse with our Heavenly Father, our Saviour, our Friend, our Brother, which is to endure throughout eternity?

Meanwhile His eye is upon us, noting with pity the irksomeness and toil of "the prayer of faith." If to all humble, trustful prayer is attached the promise: "Ask, and you shall receive," who shall tell the superadded force of that supplication which, like His own under the olive trees, perseveres in the midst of fear, and heaviness, and sorrow! "And being in an agony He prayed the longer."

---

1   Faber.

O my Saviour and my Model, unite my heaviness and my pain with Thine. Support my weak prayer at all times by the strength of Thine own. Give it the fortitude of Thine in face of a coming trial. Give it the trust that leaves all in the Father's hands, accepting as good, and best, and infinitely loving, whatever He shall ordain; saying with Thee, "Not my will, but Thine be done. Yea, Father, for so hath it seemed good in Thy sight."

Oblation and Petition, p. 82.

Prayer before a Crucifix, p. 12.

THE WELCOME OF A SUPPLIANT

III

"Good Master!"

Before Communion

THE RULER in the Gospel was mistaken in thinking that only on the spot could Christ work the cure he asked. But he was not mistaken in believing that with Him all good would come under his roof. Hence his earnest request that He would "come down" and heal his child. It was a desire that would take no refusal.

Jesus therefore said to him: "Unless you see signs and wonders, you believe not." The ruler saith to Him: "Lord, come down before that my son die." As if he would say: "Lord, in Thy kindness defer to a more seasonable hour the reproaches I so well deserve; but now look only to my need; make haste to help me.

I cannot afford that Thou shouldst seek any plea for the exercise of Thy mercy beyond my necessity and my pain."

I too, dear Lord, am right in believing that with Thy Blessed Presence all good will come into my soul. Thou art the Supreme Good. Goodness is Thy very nature. It was Thy goodness that attracted to Thee the needy and the suffering during the three-and-thirty years of Thy life on earth. A young man comes running up, and kneeling before Thee says: "Good Master, what shall I do that I may receive life everlasting?" Thou hadst just been embracing and blessing the little children. Had he seen Thee fondling the little tender things, and learned thus Thy love for the young? Anyway, he came running to pour out the fullness of his eager heart. As he looked up into Thy face, it was its goodness that struck him; the name that rose to his lips was: "Good Master." "And Jesus looking on him, loved him." Good Master, look on me and love me. I have not seen Thee yet, I have not come under the spell of Thy divine attractiveness. I am not eager, fervent, generous. But I come to Thee. I come like the ruler with a prayer for help, that no sense of my unworthiness can check. I come like the young man with desires that Thou Thyself hast kindled. And, Lord, if Thou wilt but look on me and speak to me, I will not go away sorrowful, but with Thy help will give Thee all Thou askest of me.

"Our soul waiteth for the Lord, for He is our Helper and Protector" (Ps. 32:20).

"For in Him our heart shall rejoice, and in His holy Name we have trusted" (*Ibid.*).

"Let thy mercy, O Lord, be upon us, as we have hoped in Thee" (*Ibid.*).

"How Thou deliverest them that wait for Thee, O Lord" (Ecclus. 51:12).

"I am poor and needy, and my heart is troubled within me" (Ps. 108:22).

"O look upon me and have mercy on me . . . show me a token for good" (Ps. 85:16).

"Do it for Thy Name's sake" (Jer. 14:7).

After Communion

"Holy, Holy, Holy, Lord God of Hosts!"

"We praise Thee; we bless Thee; we adore Thee; we glorify Thee."

"We give Thee thanks for Thy great glory," and more thanks for the wonderful condescension wherewith Thou dost abase Thyself to us.

"Whence is this to me that my Lord should come to me?"

"Profoundly I adore Thee, O hidden Deity."
"Truly Thou art a hidden God" (Isa. 45:15).

"Thou art Christ, the Son of the living God."

"My Lord and my God."

"Thou art worthy, O Lord our God, to receive glory, and honour, and power" (Apoc. 4:11).

"Amen. Benediction, and glory, and thanksgiving, honour, and power, and strength to our God for ever and ever. Amen" (Apoc. 7:12).

"And now, O Lord, think of me" (Tobias 3:3).

Remember Thou hast said: "Every one that asketh, receiveth" (Luke 11:10). The promise is made, not to Saints, but to "every one"; not to merit, but to prayer. I come in under every one. Give me a kind hearing, dear Lord.

I believe that as Thou art Almighty, and canst help me in every need, and All Wise, knowing the best time and way to come to my aid, so Thou art All Good and wilt help, if not always as I desire and as soon as I desire, yet always in the way best for me, as I shall see and own with joyful gratitude some day. It may well be that the grant of my prayer in the exact form that I ask would be less conducive to Thy glory and my good or the good of those for whom I pray, than that way of Thine foreseen from eternity as the best. Therefore, O Father, I commit all to Thee. I trust in Thy promise: "What I do Thou knowest not now, but thou shalt know hereafter."

I believe firmly that when at Thy feet in Heaven I look back on these things of time, and Thou discoverest to me causes and reasons hidden from me now, I shall see with admiration and delight that all has been for the best, that Thy Wisdom and Thy Love have ordered all things sweetly. To Angels and to Saints, to all the host of Heaven my cry of praise will go forth: "He hath done all things well" (Mark 7:37). "Give praise to our God, all ye His servants, and you that fear Him, little and great" (Apoc. 19:5). "As it hath pleased the Lord, so is it done" (Job 1:21). "Blessed be the Name of His majesty for ever" (Ps. 71:19).

My inability at present to guess how this will come to pass is no trial to my faith. Far easier is it to believe in the narrowness of my own views, than to doubt of the breadth, and wisdom, and goodness of Thine, my God. Why, then, should I not rehearse the praise of that first hour in Heaven; why not say now in faith and in trust: "He hath done all things well. Bless the Lord, O my soul, and let all that is within me bless His holy Name. For He hath done all things well. Bless the Lord, O my soul, and never forget all He hath done for thee. For He hath done all things well."

The time for merit will soon be past. There will be no place for faith and trust when in Thy light I shall see light. I shall not be able then to glorify Thee as now when I see in a dark manner and have the blessing of those who have not seen and have believed. Now is the acceptable time, now are the days of salvation. Therefore, dear Father, take even my most earnest desires and prayers as subject always and perfectly to Thy good pleasure. And give me such childlike trust in Thee that it may not be shaken or troubled when my prayer goes apparently unheard. "Let not your heart be troubled. You believe in God, believe also in Me," were Thy words to the Twelve at the Last Supper, and not to them only, but to all who should believe in Thee. Lord, I believe. I believe in Thee because Thou art God. I believe in Thy tender love and care of me and of all whom I love. Therefore my heart shall not be troubled. "But I will always hope; and will add to all Thy praise" (Ps. 70:14). Hope is praise, a glorious worship of Thee reserved for earth, unknown even in the Land of Praise. I will offer it gladly whilst I can. I will sing to the Lord as long as I live: I will sing praise to my God while I have my being (Ps.103:33).

Oblation and Petition, pp. 160, 162.

Prayer before a Crucifix, p. 12.

THE WELCOME OF LOVE

THE WELCOME OF LOVE

I

"Love is the fulfilling of the law"—Rom. 13:10.

RABBONI, Master, come to me and teach my heart to love Thee! Teach me this science which alone suffices, the acquisition of which discharges every obligation, and satisfies the whole intellect as well as the whole heart of man. Let life's joys and sorrows come and go; let its events and vicissitudes guided by Thy Providence pass over my head; let its experiences train, and its various influences mould my soul in conformity with the design in Thy eternal mind. And let love be the goal of all, everything converging to that centre; everything, however opposed thereto in outward seeming, tending thither—weakness, failure, imperfection, misery, past sin even—all things, all things without exception working together for the good of one who loves Thee, Lord, who desires to love Thee to the full extent of Thy commandment; who would have the whole heart, the whole soul, mind, and strength, and memory, and imagination anchored on Thee, filled with Thee, acting for Thee alone.

I think my prayer for love grows in sincerity as I realise more and more the conditions of love—the necessity of the ceaseless struggle with self which stands upon my threshold and bars Thy way into my soul, of the painful purification of the soul and the destruction of all that opposes the reign of love. To pray for love is to pray for strength in a lifelong combat. Am I ready for this, can I pray for this? Yes, Lord, even though I am conscious of such weakness as would crush all hope out of my soul, did I not know that strength is made perfect in infirmity. Abyss calleth upon abyss; from the depths I cry to Thee. Thine arm is not shortened, nor am I the only creature of Thy hands beyond the reach of Thy Omnipotence. Thou hast loved me with an everlasting love. Purify this soul of mine that before the sands of life are run out its every affection may be centred in Thee.

"And He went up and lay upon the child, and put his mouth upon his mouth, and his eyes upon his eyes, and his hands upon his hands, and the child's flesh grew warm" (4 Kings 4:34).

Christ unites His sacred flesh to mine, His Heart and Soul to mine in a union only surpassed in intimacy by the Hypostatic union itself. Gradually His life passes into mine, my coldness, inertness, lifelessness give way—"the child's flesh grew warm."

Lord, what can I do to aid in this resurrection? What but yield myself to Thee. For the work must be Thine. Only let there be nothing in me to hinder Thine action, no deliberate sin, no resistance to grace, no holding back from Thee a sacrifice Thou demandest of me. Make me more and more Thine each day. So act and influence through me, that there may be simply Thy action with nothing of mine to spoil it. Unite me so intimately with Thyself in Holy Communion, that Thy thoughts, ways, feelings, tastes, may pass into me, that I may grow into Thy likeness. Then I shall be able to work for Thee, or rather then Thou wilt be able to use me as Thy instrument. Thou didst say, dear Lord, of Thyself: "He that sent Me is with Me, and He hath not left Me alone." This is what I want to say. Let this be true of me. I am Thy ambassador sent into this world with a work to do for Thee, a work in my own soul, a work for others. Thou knowest I can do neither except in Thy strength, by Thee and with Thee. Be with me, then, always. Do not leave me alone. Oh, that by union with Thee I could say like Thee: "I do always the things that please Him."

Remember, Lord, Thy promise: "He that eateth Me, the same also shall live by Me." This is all I ask or desire—to live by Thee; Thy memory, not mine; Thy understanding, not mine; Thy will, not mine; not my thoughts, and actions, and words, but Thy thoughts, Thy words, Thy actions, the desires of Thy Soul, the affections of Thy Heart. Ah, Lord, if it could come to this at last—that Thy Spirit could flow into me and give life to me as the vine gives life to the branch!

After Communion

Thy blessed Name, dear Lord, is all I need in the first moments after Communion:

It is faith and adoration when I say—Jesus, Jesus!
It is praise and thanksgiving when I say—Jesus, Jesus!
It means hope and trust when I say—Jesus, Jesus!
It is love and welcome when I say—Jesus, Jesus!
It is sorrow for my sins when I say—Jesus, Jesus!
It is joy and delight in Thee when I say—Jesus, Jesus!
I make reparation for the outrages offered Thee when I say—Jesus, Jesus!

I abandon myself and all I have to Thee when I say—Jesus, Jesus!

I pray for union of mind and heart with Thee when I say—Jesus, Jesus!

I express all I desire for time and eternity when I say—Jesus, Jesus!

I have Thee here, I hold Thee within my narrow heart, O immense, illimitable God! I, poor and weak, possess Thee, the Creator of heaven and earth, and of all things visible and invisible. I, dull and ignorant, am one with Thee who knowest all things, past, present, and to come; all the secrets of nature and of grace; all things actual and possible; all the most hidden recesses of my heart, its sinfulness and its merits, its efforts and its frailty, its capabilities and its desires. I, cold and selfish, embrace Thee, the Lover of all that Thou hast made, the tender, steadfast Lover of my soul. Oh, that I could make Thee a return of love such as is due to Thee and might bear some proportion to Thy love of me! I could almost be content to be poor and weak and dull and ignorant, if I were not so cold. This is the pain I lift perpetually to Thee in prayer. This, if anything, would make me desire to be dissolved and be with Christ. I look forward to the time when, at the sight of Thy beauty and Thy lovableness, my coldness will melt and vanish faster than a glacier beneath the torrid sun; when, without effort—nay, impelled by the force of every power within me—I shall love Thee with all my heart, with all my soul, with all my mind, and with all my strength. *Adveniat regnum tuum!*

Lord, teach me to love Thee. Let my love grow with each Communion till it becomes a faint reflection of Thy love for me. Let me centre all my affections, desires, interests, in Thee, so that I may come at last to be like Thee in tastes and ways, and habits of thought, and mode of dealing with others. Make it easy to me to speak to Thee. In joy or trouble or uncertainty let my first thought be to consult Thee. Let me bring to Thee all that interests me, and let me take much to heart whatever interests Thee and concerns Thy glory. Help me to receive from Thy hand with unquestioning trust all that Thou permittest to befall me; to make sacrifices for Thee readily, even joyously; to be glad to suffer in Thy company, glad of the conformity with Thee which the cross brings.

My heart, dear Lord, is cold and selfish. So was the world when Thou camest to it. But what a change Thy coming made! Not all at once, but steadily, a marvellous transformation came about. Thou hadst cast fire upon it, Thy consuming love for God and man. And the flame spread and is spreading, and all who are Thine are called to feed and extend it. But to warm other hearts our own must be aglow. Warm mine, O Lord, by contact with Thine own!

Oblation and Petition, p. 82.

Prayer before a Crucifix, p. 12.

THE WELCOME OF LOVE

II

"Let this mind be in you which was also in Christ Jesus"
—Philip. 2:5.

Before Communion

A COMPREHENSIVE desire and prayer, worthy of St. Paul. Lord Jesus, could it be fulfilled in me, I would ask nothing more for myself in this life or in the next. Could it be realised in those I love, in those entrusted to me, in all Christians, in all men—there would be nothing left for us to desire. Could the whole human family, of which Thou art the Head, live by Thy life and Thy spirit, what more would there be to hope for—Thy Will would be done on earth as it is in heaven: Thy Kingdom would have come: the kingdom of this world would have "become our Lord's and His Christ's" (Apoc. 11:15).

Our work in life is to bring our mind and heart, our inward dispositions and exterior actions, into conformity with those of Christ. His predilections and aversions; His valuation of the comforts, pleasures and honours of this passing life; His judgments respecting poverty, persecution for justice' sake, meekness, mourning, deeds of mercy, forgiveness of injuries; His estimate of the Cross in its many shapes, of treasure in heaven that faileth not; His tenderness for the little children and the weak things of this world, for the outcast, and the fallen, and the downtrodden; His love for His sinless Mother; His all-absorbing love of the Father, which, to use our human language, was the ruling passion of His Soul, which, when His Heart was fullest, freest and heaviest, found vent in the most vehement words of His sacred lips—all this is the translation to us of the mind of Christ. Well might the great Apostle who had so well "learned Christ," content himself with this one desire for the children whom he had begotten in the Gospel: "Let this mind be in you which was in Christ Jesus."

Why should not this desire be realised in me after Communion, after my frequent Communions? For what does Christ come to me if not for this? O Jesus, take from my mind what has no place in Thine, and give me to live by Thee!

Let me be united with Thee as love desires in thought, affection and will, abiding in Thee and Thou in me. Give me the strong purpose of overcoming in myself all that is displeasing to Thee and a hindrance to Thy love, and help me, for without Thee I can do nothing. Destroy the selfishness that crowds Thee out of my soul and stifles whatever of generosity may be there. Make me ready for labour and for sacrifice in Thy service, ready to give Thee gifts that cost. Give me grace to shun all willful offence of Thee; to desire and to choose what best pleases Thee; to love Thee with my whole mind, directing to Thee all my thoughts, intentions, actions; with my whole heart, fixing on Thee all my affections, seeking Thy glory, promoting Thy interests; with my whole soul and all its desires and aspirations; with my whole strength. In a word, let Thy mind be in me, O Lord!

AFTER COMMUNION

"Bless the Lord, all ye His Angels, you that are mighty in strength" (Ps. 102:20). "Sing praises to our God, sing ye; sing praises to our King, sing ye" (Ps. 46:7). "For this is God, our God unto eternity, and for ever and ever" (Ps. 47:15):

Who became incarnate for my sake:

Who was born in Bethlehem—for me:

Who grew up in the Home at Nazareth, and was subject to His parents, and toiled at a trade:

"Jesus, at whose Name every knee shall bow" (Philip. 2:10).

"Bless the Lord, all ye servants of the Lord" (Ps.133:1). "O magnify the Lord with me, and let us extol His Name together" (Ps. 33:4). For this is God, our God unto eternity, and for ever and ever:

Who lived in a despised village for thirty years — for me:

Who suffered hunger and thirst, and cold, and weariness—for me:

Who went to and fro among men, gentle, attractive, doing good to all:

Jesus, meek and humble of heart.

"Come, let us praise the Lord with joy, let us joyfully sing to God, our Saviour" (Ps. 94:1). For this is God, our God unto eternity, and for ever and ever:

Who gathered together the Twelve and founded His Church—for me:

Who healed the blind, and the maimed, and lepers, and every disease and every infirmity:

Who welcomed and absolved the outcast sinner:

Jesus, who came to seek and to save that which was lost.

"Let the mercies of the Lord give glory to Him, and His wonderful works to the children of men" (Ps. 106:8). For this is God, our God unto eternity, and for ever and ever:

Who for my sake became a worm and no man;

Who loved me and delivered Himself for me even to the death of the Cross:

Who rose from the dead—for me:

Who stands at the right hand of the Father, ever making intercession for me:

Who will be my reward exceeding great:

Jesus, yesterday, and today, and the same for ever.

"Bless the Lord, O my soul, and let all that is within me bless His holy Name" (Ps. 102:1).

"Bless the Lord, O my soul, and never forget all He hath done for thee" (*Ibid.*).

"Thou art worthy, O Lord our God, to receive glory, and honour, and power" (Apoc. 4:11).

Amen. Benediction and glory, and thanksgiving, honour, and power, and strength to our God for ever and ever. Amen" (Apoc. 7:12).

Lord, I should love to make Thee loved! I envy those who by the holiness of their life, the influence of their example, the sweet tactfulness of their ways, light up the fire of Thy love on every side of their path through life. But why should not this be the fruit of my Communions? Every branch, even the farthest and the feeblest, is vivified by the parent vine, and Thou hast said: "I am the vine, you the branches; he that abideth in Me and I in him, the same beareth much fruit." There is no other condition. The promise is not to mature sanctity, heroic self-sacrifice, sublime heights of prayer, but to abiding in Thee. But Thy words imply frequent union; a Communion at distant intervals is not abiding. If I want to bear much fruit, if I want to live by Thee, I must come to Thee often.

And in how many ways dost Thou urge upon me this frequent reception:

"Come to Me, all you that labour."

"Come, eat My bread, and drink the wine that I have mingled for you."

"You will not come to Me that you may have life."

"Compel them to come in, that My house may be full."

"Unless you eat the flesh of the Son of Man and drink His blood, you shall not have life in you."

Invitations, threats, reproaches—all pressed into the service of love, all testifying to Thy eagerness, O Divine Host! Thou must see Thy house full, Thy table crowded with guests. Are we necessary, then, to

Thy happiness? In a sense, yes, for God is love.

Lord, I will come to Thee; I have stayed away too long. I will come to Thee often that I may live by Thee. Let my thoughts be the reflection of Thine, my words the echo of Thine, my deeds the continuation of Thine. Let my thoughts about the events of this passing life be lofty like Thine; about the failings of others, tender and compassionate like Thine; about my own weakness and misery, patient, hopeful of all things, like Thine. As the vine vivifies the branch, as the head gives life, and movement, and direction to the least of the members, so be to me, Thy last and least, the principle of spiritual life and energy, that all my works may be done in and by Thee, and may profit the souls whom Thou love.

Oblation and Petition, pp. 160, 162.

Prayer before a Crucifix, p. 12.

THE WELCOME OF LOVE

III

"I sought Him whom my soul loveth"—Cant. 3:1.

Before Communion

THE first word of our catechism puts before us the end of our creation, the one only reason for which we were created and sent into this world—God to know; God to love and serve; to know, that I may be able to love and serve. This is my business in life. It is for this life is given. And when the time allotted me for this work has run its course, the life that is lent me will be called for again (Wisd. 15:8).

Without this end, my life here is meaningless and inexplicable. The powers of my soul, unless I misdirect them, are ever tending to God. Prayer, in which they all concur, is feeling for Him in the night; seeking a way to His presence; waiting at His door;

trying one entrance after another; hastening to where a ray of light from the Throne room falling out on the darkness, tells of a chink through which I may perchance catch a glimpse of Him.

Oh, it is weary work, this waiting, and listening, this eagerness disappointed! Harder still the waiting and listening when eagerness has died out and stern will alone continues the quest for Him, or sits down dogged but uncomforted at His door!

Weary work in truth, yet more contenting than any happiness outside of God. For we are made for Him, and a lifelong search is more satisfying to the soul than the finding and possession of aught that is not Himself.

In the Canticle of Canticles, the history of love, we find this search depicted, with its diligence, its disappointments, its questionings, its perseverance, its final reward. "In the night I sought Him whom my soul loveth, I sought Him and found Him not. . . . Have you seen Him whom my soul loveth? . . . When I had a little passed by I found Him whom my soul loveth, I found Him, and will not let Him go." (Cant. 3:1). "My Beloved to me and I to Him, till the day break and the shadows retire" (Cant. 2:16-17).

So let me see Thee, Lord, through the night of this life, watching, listening, questioning, where the

beautiful things of the physical world, and the events
of daily life, and the inspirations of grace are ready
to reveal Thee to me. Give me the eager heart, O
Lord, from which, though Thou mayst hide Thyself
for a time, Thou wilt not withhold Thyself at last.
Remember Thou hast said, "Every one that asketh
receiveth, and he that seeketh, findeth; and to him that
knocketh, it shall be opened." I ask; I seek; I knock.
Open to me, not only the door of Thy kingdom, but
Thy arms and Thy heart, and say to me—"Come!"

After Communion

*"I believe, Lord, and falling down
he adored Him."—John 9:38*

"Lord, I believe, I adore."

"Thou art Christ, the Son of the Living God"
(John 11:27).

"My Lord and my God" (John 20:28).

"What have I in heaven? and besides Thee what
do I desire upon earth? Thou art the God of my heart
and the God that is my portion for ever" (Ps. 72:25).

"Sing to the Lord, O ye His Saints" (Ps. 29:5).

"For who is God but the Lord, or who is God but
our God?" (Ps. 17:32).

"Let all Thy works, O Lord, praise Thee, and let
Thy Saints bless Thee" (Ps. 144:10).

Lord, teach me to love Thee. Draw me within the circle of Thy attraction. Do for me what Thou hast done for so many. There are hearts that were once dull and irresponsive like mine, hoping they loved, but conscious that in their affection there was no spark of the glowing fire that burned in the breast of Thy Saints. They desired to love, to make Thee a return for the infinite love wherewith Thou hadst loved them. They prayed for this; prayed with difficulty; prayed against repugnance; prayed coldly, wearily—but prayed. Years came and went, and still their dry, hard prayer went up to God. Nothing came of it, no change, no greater facility, no warmth in their relations with Him, no greater ease in the sacrifices His service called for. So it seemed. And still they prayed on, little dreaming that the very perseverance of their joyless prayer for love was love's choicest fruit: "Lord, teach me to love Thee; teach me to love Thee." Not yet was it safe for Him to show them how truly they loved. Death came, and they met Him for the first time, met Him face to face. His arms were outstretched; His face was glowing; His eye lit up at their approach, and ere they could fall at His feet. He had folded them to His heart. "Lord, Thou knowest that I love Thee," they had said below, diffidently, as if fearing a disclaimer. Now He shows them their love purified as gold fire-tried. They see it, they recognise it now. All Heaven bears witness to it and congratulates them on their fidelity to Him, "whom having not seen they loved" (1 Pet. 1:8). All Heaven rejoices with them in their nearness to Him for all eternity, in the eternal vision of Him, the eternal embrace of Him that is the reward of earth's sorely tried, suffering, yet clinging love.

Who would not be content to wait for reward such as this! Lord, I will wait as long as Thou willest, and through any trial that Thou willest. I will wait patiently, for if Thou delayest Thou wilt surely come.

And Thou, dearest Lord, wilt be patient too. Thou wilt wait for me, bearing with my sluggishness, my selfishness, my trying ways. It will not be for long. Life here will soon be done, and then—Life everlasting! Even in Purgatory there will be the perfect fulfilling of the great commandment. It will be Purgatory only because it will keep me from Him whom I love. Heaven will be Heaven because its first instant of revelation of the King in His beauty will bring a capacity for, and an endowment of, love such as I have never dreamed of here; a love that will fill

to overflowing, absorb and satisfy through an endless
eternity the soul Thou hast made for Thyself.

Oblation and Petition, p. 82.

Prayer before a Crucifix, p. 12.

SA CONFIANCE L'A SAUVÉ

ENNUIS   TENTATIONS   DÉSESPOIRS   MALADIES

THE WELCOME
OF A CROSS-BEARER

THE WELCOME OF A
CROSS-BEARER

I

"Lord, he whom Thou lovest is sick"—John 11:3.

HOW our Lord tries His friends, and how He expects them to trust Him! He was beyond the Jordan, in the place where John baptized, when a messenger came from the sisters at Bethany to tell Him of the sickness of their brother: "Lord, he whom Thou lovest is sick." It was a trustful message, a mere representation of their need, no request for Him to come to them, still less any urgent solicitation. It was trustful, and it was considerate. They only reminded Him that the trouble concerned one whom He loved. The bearer of the tidings waited to see if our Lord would return with him, and interrupt, as was

His wont, His work of teaching to go to a house of mourning. No. "When He had heard therefore that he was sick, He still remained in the same place two days." We are not even told of any message of comfort to the sisters. All He said was: "This sickness is not unto death, but for the glory of God, that the Son of God may be glorified by it."

From Bethany to Perea was an eight hours' journey, and the man must have been a day on the road. Our Lord stayed yet two days in Perea before returning to Judea, and on His arrival found that Lazarus had been four days in the grave. Consequently he must have died soon after the departure of the messenger, and would have been buried in about two hours.

What were the thoughts of Martha and Mary as, barefoot and covered with their long black veils, they sat on the ground bewailing their dead after the manner of mourning among the Jews? There was plenty of unhelpful sympathy. For "many came to comfort them concerning their brother," and to express surprise that the great Wonder-worker who showed Himself so prodigal of His favours to strangers had been unable to do anything for His friends. The stricken sisters listened in silence. What could they say? Their Lord had not come or taken any notice of their trouble beyond the mysterious words that the sickness was not unto death; and temptation, always busy about those in sorrow, whispered: This, then, was the great prophet in whom they had put their trust. He did not seem greatly concerned for them or to understand much about the case. At the hour when He said the sickness was not unto death, Lazarus was already dead.

How did Martha and Mary meet the trial from within and without? How did they keep up each other's trust? They could not fathom our Lord's words that this sickness was for the glory of God, and that the Son of God might be glorified by it. His ways were "past finding out." But they clung to Him in their desolation. They thought of His tenderness in the past, and over and over again kept repeating that if He had been there Lazarus had not died. These were the first words that came to their lips when He came at last, and they threw themselves at His feet. The loving reproach brought tears to His eyes, though He knew the time was at hand for Him to turn their sorrow into joy.

Now He need not have let them suffer so sorely these four days. A word enabling them to penetrate the meaning of His words on receiving their message would have been so easy. Is any reason given why He left them for awhile in their desolation? Yes:

"Now Jesus loved Martha, and her sister Mary, and Lazarus. When He had heard therefore that He was sick, He still remained in the same place two days" (John 11:5-6). An artificer employs for his work the tools proper to it. For the sanctification of souls God uses the instrument by which the Author of their salvation was Himself perfected (Heb. 2). His ways of dealing with them are infinitely varied, but we find none that has passed through life without its cross. Nothing can supply the place of the cross or do its work. Where it stays long and is well received, it chastens, strengthens, ennobles. It gives a refinement, a spiritual perception, a depth, a maturity, not found in souls that have come but slightly under its discipline. It is the cross that develops all the possibilities of human nature. But wherever it is present, God is there, watching to see that its pressure is neither too heavy nor too prolonged. Our Lord yearned for the moment when He might go to comfort those whom He loved. There is an eagerness in His words to the Twelve: "Let us go into Judea again....I am glad for your sakes that I was not there, but let us go to him."

"Let us go to him." Say this today, dear Lord, as Thou comest to me. I welcome Thee to a sad heart, but one that clings to Thee in its pain, accepts Thy Will, enters into Thy designs, trusts Thee to bring good out of this as out of every trial. All things work together unto good to them that love Thee. I love Thee; Lord, Thou knowest that I love Thee. I know that the cross brings with it the opportunity of showing a purer and more generous love. I know that amid pain, which entered into every fibre of soul and body, Thou didst prove Thy love for me. Take my pain, my willing acceptance of the cross that weighs upon me now, as proof of my love. By the tenderness of Thy Heart, by Thy tears over the grave of Lazarus, draw me closer to Thee by this trial and by every trial of my life.

"Where have you laid him?"
"Lord, come and see."
A friend must see and hear everything that concerns us. Nothing is too insignificant for his notice. Everything will go better for his advice. If our orchids have won a prize, he must admire them. If we have fallen out with a neighbour, he must hear how it came about. If our hearts are breaking over another grave, he must come and see where we have laid him. "I have called you friends," our Lord says to us. He values the confidence that counts on His

friendship in the least affairs of everyday life as in its crucial hours. And he invites it. "What are these discourses that you hold one with another as you walk, and are sad?"

It is hard to bring home to ourselves what He must have been to those who during His life on earth He called His friends, what it was to be able to fall back on an affection that was omnipotent, all-wise, unfailingly tender and provident. With Him at hand no harm could come. Hence the trustful word of Martha and Mary: "Lord, if Thou hadst been here my brother had not died." He inspired a trust that no apparent rigour could shake. If He seemed deaf to their prayers, He had some good reason for refusal or delay; greater good would come to them in the end. Whatever came must be not good only but best, if it was His choice for them. And so disappointed hopes brought no diminution of trust. It only meant that He was going to help in some better way. "Lord, if Thou hadst been here my brother had not died. But now also I know that whatsoever Thou wilt ask of God, God will give it Thee." "It is not good to take the bread from the children, and cast it to the dogs," was His answer to the Canaanite who followed Him with her imploring: "Lord, help me." "Yea, Lord," she replied, and adroitly turned his objection into a further plea for mercy.

Oh, that we could count on Him as did the friends of His life on earth! That we could learn to bring all our troubles to His feet. He does not mind if our tale is one-sided; if we give our own faulty version only, bearing all over it the unmistakable varnish of self-love. It is the confidence He values, the outpouring that gives Him the opportunity of infusing His own Spirit into ours, "pouring in oil and wine," the soothing and strengthening grace we need. We shall never leave His feet without the soreness of our wounds being to some extent allayed, the chafing of our cross lessened, the will braced to follow our Master with greater courage on the uphill road.

After Communion

"Salvation to our God who sitteth upon the throne—the throne of His glory in Heaven, the throne here on earth of my poor heart."

"O ye Angels of the Lord, bless the Lord, praise and exalt Him above all for ever."

"Give praise to our God, all ye His servants: and you that fear Him, little and great."

"O give thanks to the Lord, because He is good, because His mercy endureth for ever."

"And now, O Lord, think of me" (Tobias 3:3).

I come to Thee as the sisters of Bethany came after their brother's death. They had done all that lay in them to avert the blow. They had used all human means; they had prayed; they had waited patiently, looking for Thy help. And the blow fell. Their hearts were crushed, but there was no rebellion, no repining. They wondered at Thy ways, but adored what they could not fathom. They looked not to creatures for consolation, but betook themselves to Thee, and falling down at Thy feet poured out their sad hearts in the same words: "Lord, if Thou hadst been here my brother had not died." They knew that Thou art all-powerful, yet there is no petition. Others came asking for miracles, and their faith is rewarded. Martha and Mary, who know Thee better than most, ask nothing. They had taken their trouble meekly from Thy hand, they lay it now at Thy feet, and look up into Thy face and trust. This won more from Thee than the most fervent prayer. And may we not say that the like trust will win more from Thee now? Nay, Lord, may we not believe that we in our troubles have a claim upon Thee that Martha and Mary had not? It was incomparably more easy to trust Him, whom they knew and loved as a personal Friend, than to rely on One whom we have not seen as yet, whom we know by hearsay, not face to face. And therefore the merit will be greater. Where sense has no foothold, faith needs to walk with firmer step, to cling more persistently to Thee. "Because thou hast seen Me, Thomas, thou hast believed: blessed are they who have not seen, and have believed." Blessed, dear Lord, by Thine own lips are those who have not seen Thee, yet trust as Martha and Mary trusted; who bring their sorrow to Thine altar, and leave it to Thee, the Hidden God, to help when and as Thou wilt—by removing the chalice from them, or by strengthening them to drink it generously after Thee and for Thy sake.

Oblation and Petition, pp. 160, 162.

Prayer before a Crucifix, p. 12.

THE WELCOME OF A CROSS-BEARER

II

"Give us help in trouble, for vain is the aid of man"
—Ps. 59:13.

BEFORE COMMUNION

VAIN is the aid of man—not from want of patience to hear, or effort to unravel, or sympathy to appreciate difficulties, or kindness to seek and suggest a remedy. Goodwill we find abundantly, more than we have any right to expect. But there are times and needs when it goes for very little, how little we dare not show.

Yes, truly, vain is the aid of man. He alone can bring true help in trouble who understands us through and through—every fibre and fold of our complex nature; every influence that has been brought to bear upon it from the beginning; every response of will that has gone to the moulding of our character for better or for worse. Who knows our immense possibilities for good and for evil; the precise amount of guilt and of merit attaching to our every thought, and word, and deed, since we came to the use of reason. Who sees the ignorance and frailty that enables Him to find such abundant excuse for us; and the goodwill He is so ready to magnify and reward. Our bringing up He knows, and how home and friends, reading, amusements, the conflicts, cares, and sorrows of life have left their mark upon us. He understands our peculiar temperament, and estimates with perfect accuracy our strength and our resources, our physical, moral, and spiritual deficiencies. The pressure put upon spirits and temper by the monotony of daily duties and the rubs of daily life is known to Him, and the heavier trial of anxiety for those we love. The exact nature of our spiritual difficulties, and the causes of phenomena and vicissitudes that are altogether beyond our ken, are clear to Him. How it comes to pass that darkness suddenly overclouds our soul, as a fog drops upon the sea; why grace will bear us triumphantly through one trial, and in another leave us to feel the effects of our own weakness and insufficiency, is His secret, who orders all things sweetly. He knows the precise degree of grace here and of glory hereafter that He wills us to attain, and where we further His designs and where we thwart them.

We watch the gnats at play on a summer evening, but our eye cannot follow the intricacies of their mazy dance. Not so is it with us and the God who made us. Down every path we wander from the cradle to the grave, through all the network of manifold and conflicting influences under which we come, His eye follows us with unwearying interest, and a solicitude unimaginable in its tenderness. Whatever sways us from without, whatever charms or chafes, the complex processes of thought, the play of imagination, the ebb and flow of passion, the deliberate acts of choice—all the crossing and recrossing and seeming tangle of the threads of life, stands out before Him clear and distinct, with its bearing on the destiny evolved therefrom by the action of our will, in the exercise of its dread but glorious prerogative of freedom.

Oh, surely, we may turn with confidence to such a One as this! For He is not Creator only, though this were sweet enough, but Father and Friend. He not only knows, but feels, and loves, and provides. If He lets the goodwill of those about us fail so signally to bring us help in trouble, it is that we may be driven into His open arms and folded to His breast. He needs none to disclose to Him the secrets of hearts, for He knows what is in man. He hath set His eye upon our hearts (Ecclus. 17:7), and every heart is understood by Him (Ecclus. 16:20).

Musicians strain and snap at times the strings of their instruments. They overestimate their capabilities and their power of resistance. But the far more delicate instrument of the human soul has never yet been strained beyond endurance by the hand of its Creator. He knows it through and through, its powers, its limitations, its every vibration of joy and pain. He who will not break the bruised reed has never riven the living fibres of "the harps of God" (Apoc. 15:20). Nay more. He never puts them to any tension except to bring them into harmony for the heavenly concert with which they are to mingle, the eternal *Magnificat* in which each has its appointed part. Do we want to be left out? Do we refuse our training? Are we going to be rebellious beneath His touch, or find it too exacting or too prolonged? Do we want to be flung aside where there is never-ending discord, "no order, but everlasting horror" (Job 10:22)?

My God, I give myself up into Thy hands. Oh, if I knew for what Thou hast created this soul of mine, what melody Thou canst draw from this work of Thy hands, with what trembling ecstasy should I surrender

myself to Thee to be prepared for the part I am to take
in the hymn of praise that creation is to sing to Thee
when time is done!

After Communion

"Blessed be the Lord for this day" (3 Kings 5:7).

"Bless the Lord, O my soul, and never forget all
He hath done for thee" (Ps. 102:2).

"Give praise to our God, all ye His servants: and
you that fear him, little and great" (Apoc. 19:5).

"Praise ye the Lord, for He is good; sing ye to His
Name, for it is sweet" (Ps. 134:3).

"For He hath satisfied the empty soul, and hath
filled the hungry soul with good things" (Ps. 106:9).

"Thou art worthy, O Lord our God, to receive
glory, and honour, and power" (Apoc. 4:11).

"Amen. Benediction, and glory, and thanksgiving,
honour, and power, and strength to our God for ever
and ever. Amen" (Apoc. 7:12).

Lord, come to me today to teach me how to take
all things straight from Thy hand, not bemoaning
myself, not blaming others when trouble comes. This
is what the world does. This is its way of taking what
it calls failure and misfortune. But Thy servants
look at things from a higher standpoint. They know

that He who created them out of love, and in His love has prepared for them an eternity of delights without one pang, or hitch, or disappointment to overcloud their happiness, expects them to trust Him in the little sorrows of this short life that will be gone directly. He wants them—not to like always what He sends—their Lord Himself did not do this, but to take it as training, sensibly and bravely, knowing it is to fit them for that life before the Throne of God, whose joy eye has not seen, nor ear heard, nor heart of man conceived.

"Remember that thou knowest not His work . . . every one beholdeth afar off" (Job 36:25). We do not, we cannot, see and understand clearly the inscrutable ways of God! But we have His promise: "What I do thou knowest not now, but thou shalt know hereafter." Faith and hope have so short a time assigned them in which to glorify Him, that there should be no waste, or faltering in their service. Of the three theological virtues, hope is the worst treated. We take ourselves to task for faults against faith and charity, but against hope we offend continually and without the smallest scruple. Yet it is enjoined us no less than the others. And it is the outcome of the other two. If faith and charity are what they should be, hope will be bright and strong. Firm belief and fervent love beget hope, as blue and yellow blending in the rainbow produce the tender green.

Can I be mistrustful of a love that dates from eternity? Can I fear harm in the shelter of the everlasting arms? Shall I be querulous or anxious when my Father's ways are "past finding out," or doubt the tenderness of Him who will have mercy more than a mother (Ecclus. 4:11)?

All comes straight from God to me, always, always, always; and if I like I may leave out the human element altogether.

All comes—therefore these very things that try me so—this special cross—this peculiar difficulty —these singularly perplexing circumstances—all.

Comes straight—no person or event intervening to divert things from their right course—but all straight from God.

From God—who knows me thoroughly—my wants—my desires—my need of purification— His designs over me—from God, my Father and the tenderest of Fathers.

To me—His child, weak, sensitive, frightened, able to bear so little—yet desiring to please Him, to satisfy Him, to conform my will to His, to return Him love for love.

Always, always, always—therefore this morning, this afternoon—in spite of circumstances that would seem to indicate that just this one thing could not have come from Him—*always, always*: "To them that love God all things work together unto good" (Rom. 8:28). How can I get out of that?

And if I like—of course I like! How should I not like the truth—like to see God wherever He is; however, He hides Himself; under any disguise, however unlikely or repulsive! Wherever He appears, amid the glories of Thabor, across the sea in the misty morning, love is quick to recognise Him and to cry: *Dominus est!* It is the Lord!

I may leave out *the human element*—oh, it is this that hurts! Like Peter on the stormy waves, we turn our eyes from Jesus to look at creatures, and trouble comes in at once, and we begin to sink. It is the human element that is the hardest part of most trials. Then why look at it? Why not leave it out of count, as I may do with perfect truth? A wife who gets a message from her husband does not stop to consider the messenger. Neither must I stop at means; the instrument is nothing to me. The notice of Him whom I love, the word that comes to me from Him, the desire to carry out His Will, absorbs me completely: *Dominus est!* It is the Lord! Lord, what wilt Thou have me to do?

O Lord my God, give me the unclouded faith that sees Thee and Thee alone in all that befalls me—in all events; in all joys and sorrows; in health and in sickness; in success and in failure; in evil report and good report; in accidents, in disappointments, in weariness, in consolation, in interior trials. And give me not only light to see Thee, but love to embrace Thee, always and everywhere, my First Beginning and my Last End, my Lord and my God!

Oblation and Petition, p. 10.

Prayer before a Crucifix, p. 12.

THE WELCOME OF A
CROSS-BEARER

III

*"Come to Me all you that labour and are burdened,
and I will refresh you"*—Matt. 11:28.

"COME"—Is it an invitation or a command?
Both. It is an invitation, for our Lord's way is
ever to attract rather than to compel. And it is a
precept, for "Except you eat the flesh of the Son of
Man and drink His blood, you shall not have life in
you" (John 6:54).

"Come to Me"—He does not send the hungry
away fasting as the Apostles would have done, when
five thousand men, besides women and children,
followed Him into the desert. "They have no need
to go," He said. And He gathered them round Him,

and fed them from His own hand, and sent them home refreshed and happy.

"*Come to Me all*"—lest in my perversity I should deem myself exempted or excluded. But His invitation and His precept admit of no exception. "Come all."

"Come to One who knows you through and through; who sees where and how the burden presses; where are the weak places in your soul; who discerns every effort and every desire; follows with loving interest every struggle, and often and often finds even in failure more to pity than to blame.

"Come to Me that I may help you, that I may guide and strengthen your hands, that I may lift your burden from you or lighten by sharing it, that I may show you the likeness to Me that it is working out in your soul, the reward it is meriting."

"Come to Me that I may make over to you My treasures; My likes and dislikes, to be the rule of yours; My peace that the world can neither give nor take away; My love that is compensation for the loss of all beside."

"Come to Me that I may comfort you in your anxiety for those you love. There is no pain in which I can give you fuller sympathy. 'I also have a heart like you' (Job 12:3). I know what it is to see evil influences telling, the will weakening, the heart growing callous, the forces of the spiritual life losing their power to check and to charm."

"Come to Me with confidence, for I am one of your race. I took a human Heart that I might know by my own experience what you have to suffer, and be able to give you that sympathy that a fellow-sufferer alone can give. The sting of injustice and ingratitude I have felt, and the agony of love powerless to save its best beloved. All that is bitterest in human sorrow I chose to feel, that I might draw to Myself by fellow-feeling every sorrowing heart."

"There are times when pent-up pain is stifling your soul. Come in those hours to Me. Unburden yourself before Me. Say all, and say it freely. The vehemence of expostulation is understood by Me. No fear of angering by intemperate words One who beholds the agony of the soul. Without check, without rebuke, it may pour itself out before the all-loving Creator, whose infinite compassion has the added tenderness of His perfect human Heart. I remember the night of the Agony in Gethsemane, when the sorrows as well as the sins of My brethren were laid upon Me. I remember the strong cry and tears of my supplication. I take up and make My own, the cry, the broken prayer, of every sufferer, and set it before the Father with the pleading merits of My Passion. I will always hear. I will always help. The help shall be release from pain if this is best for you. If I see, what you too will see some day, that fitter answer to prayer will be courage and strength, in that form your help shall come. O child, do not deprive yourself of what I can do for you in your hours of lonely trial. Come to Me and learn by your own experience the resource you have in My Heart!"

"Come to Me above all when the sense of sin oppresses you. It is a force that must impel you to Me, or from Me. What I want is that it should drive you into My arms. How is it that you fly from Me when you need Me most? That you think your faithlessness or your ingratitude should have so estranged Me or changed the relations between us as to make Me less your Father than before? When you sin you are still Mine (Wisd. 15:2). When by mortal sin a soul severs itself from Me as far as in it lies, it has not thereby made Me its enemy as men understand the word. They wish evil to their friend of an hour ago. They close their heart against him. They shrink from reconciliation. Nothing of this has place in Me. In the instant of his rejection of Me My arms are flung open to receive him again. My Heart is ready to restore all he has lost, to cherish,

and trust, and bless as before. And this not once
only, but as often as he needs and wills, not after
one fall only, but after seventy times seven. I have
loved you with an ever-lasting love, a love that is
persistent, patient, hoping all things. Come to
Me after your falls, and I will make all right again.
Come for the strength and the comfort you need.
Come for the embrace and the kiss that are waiting
for you. Come to Me quickly, if not to content your
love, to satisfy Mine."

After Communion

"Bless the Lord, all ye servants of the Lord"
(Ps. 133:1).

"Exalt ye the Lord our God" (Ps. 98:5).

"Bless the Lord, all ye His Angels" (Ps. 102:20)

"Give glory to the Lord, for He is good" (Ps. 106:1).

"Adore the Lord our God, and give thanks to
Him" (Tobias 11:7).

"Adore the Lord my God" (Dan. 14:24).

"Bless the Lord, for He hath shown His wonderful
mercy to me" (Ps. 30:22).

"My soul doth magnify the Lord, and my spirit
hath rejoiced in God my Saviour" (Luke 1:46).

"Because He that is mighty hath done great things
to me, and holy is His Name" (*Ibid.*).

"What shall I offer to the Lord that is worthy?
Wherewith shall I kneel before the high God?"
(Micheas 6:6).

"Give to the most High according to what
He hath given to thee" (Ecclus. 35:12).

Lord, Thou hast given me Thyself. I return Thee
Thyself in thanksgiving for Thy unspeakable Gift.
Thou hast given me Thy cross. I bring it to Thee to
be blessed and sanctified by Thy Presence.

My cross is all that goes against self; all that it
costs to reduce self; to bring self into conformity with
Thy Will; whatever goes counter to my liking in
companions, duties, the way things fall out, the way
things are done.

Is it more than this? Is my cross one of those heavy,
lifelong, sanctifying trials that make each day a Way
of the Cross? Lord, Thou knowest. Behold, O Lord,
Thou hast known all things . . . my path and my line
Thou hast searched out; Thou hast foreseen all my
ways (Ps. 138:4). Thou art my God, my lots are in
Thy hands (Ps. 30:16). There let my will be too.
Teach me to see as Thou seest; to take a right view
of the cross in whatever shape it comes to me. This
alone would set right my outlook on life. I know that
suffering must come to us all. I believe that it comes

by Thy Will or permission, and that it is laden with good to those who love Thee. But I want much more than this. I want to realise what I believe. I want to be intimately convinced that suffering is not what the world takes it to be—an evil, but a treasure in which those nearest and dearest to Thee have the largest share. In the lives of the Saints I see plainly that this is so. But to appreciate the value of the cross in my own life is a different matter. Let me understand as they did the good hidden in the cross. It does not sanctify all whom it touches. There are many whom it drives from Thee. Lord, let it do for me what it has done for all Thy holy ones. Let it teach me that we are wayfarers here on earth, having here no lasting city. And let it draw me to Thee. Those who were attracted to Thee during Thy life on earth were not the strong and the successful, but those in sorrow either on their own account or for those they loved. Among the suffering we always find Thee. Whilst all prospers with us we are apt to forget Thee, Lord. But a reverse, a humiliation comes, creatures fail us, and at once we betake ourselves to the Creator who is so kind that He does not reject us even then. My God, let every trial draw me closer and closer to Thee. Let it bring out Thy likeness in my soul, as the sculptor's mallet and file and chisel bring beauty out of the shapeless marble and realise his ideal at last. The work cannot be done without suffering. Lord, strengthen me to suffer. Take from me the excessive fear of everything that brings me pain. Help me to welcome pain as a means of expiating past sins, as giving me compassion for others—above all, as likening me to Thee, my Master, and enabling me to prove my love to Thee. Thy sensitive Body and Soul have sounded all the depths of human sorrow that Thou mightest be able to feel for us in every pain of body and mind. Unite my little pains with Thine that they may merit an eternal reward, the reward of special nearness to Thee in Thy Kingdom when life is done.

Oblation and Petition, p. 82.

Prayer before a Crucifix, p. 12.

THE LAST WELCOME

THE LAST WELCOME

I

"Though I should walk in the midst of the shadow of death I will fear no evils, for Thou art with me"—Ps. 22:4.

Before Communion

THE Last Welcome! When will it be, and Where, and how? All this is hidden from me. But what is certain is that it will be soon. No matter how many Communions there may be between this and my last, that last will come soon.

How fast the years speed by! How quickly the Easter Communions come round, and the First Fridays, and His visits on the great Feasts! Each strengthens my union with our Lord by fresh degrees of sanctifying grace, and confers a right to a closer union with Him hereafter. Each is a safeguard in dangers to soul and body of which I shall know nothing in this life. Each gives me a title to the guidance and the strength daily needs require, and to the special assistance necessary in critical hours. By each reception of the divine Food, our Lord verifies more and more fully His promise: "He that eats Me shall live by Me." By each I grow more and more into His likeness.

This is what I owe to the Communions of my life. But what will the last do for me? O my Lord, how much I count upon Thy last visit! How I shall need Thee to shield and support me, to prepare me for the end! But I must do my part now. I provide as far as may be for the great events of life; must I not bring preparation to the supreme act which can never be repeated, on which all depends? It is the greatest mistake to suppose that the mere fact of death being at hand will rouse me to extra exertion. The effect of the warning will be more than counterbalanced by the pain and weakness and weariness of that time. To do as well as usual and what is necessary, will be all I shall be fit for. God grant that doing as well as usual in the way of preparation for the Sacraments may be all that is necessary and more! Some people count on a long process of preparation—a general confession, and what not. Much better to get all done beforehand. I may have a long illness; I may have none. Death may come in a railway accident, a fire, without a moment's warning. I must run no risk. I must make all secure now. I will leave nothing to be said when I come to die. Each time I leave the confessional it shall be with the humble confidence that if my call were to come then, I should be ready. My God, surely there will be enough in the present and the future to tax my failing powers, without having to go back upon the past to rectify what I have deliberately postponed to the hour of death! How should I in the anguish and prostration of that time be capable of an effort I was unwilling to make in the days of my strength? I must not count on time or will, or anything except the mercy of God and the habits of life that will stand me in good stead then. For my last confession I shall want contrition, strong, humble, trusting. I must prepare it now by dwelling thoughtfully on the motives for sorrow; that when I come to die, the sight of the crucifix, a suggested word, may awaken the sorrow that is in my heart always. It is in the hour of death that God rewards the habits of life. If I am earnest now in prayer for contrition and in making use of the motives that lead to it, He will come to the help of my weakness then, and give me for my last sacramental absolution a sorrow that will not only purify my soul from guilt, but go far to cancel the debt of punishment.

My God, who art coming to me now, give me true grief of heart for everything in my life by which I have offended Thee. Let it be that perfect sorrow which grieves for having sinned against a God so good in Himself and so infinitely worthy of love. And make it perfect, not in kind only but in degree, that its effect may be not remission of guilt only but of the pain sin has deserved. There is no grace I ask more earnestly than this—an abiding sorrow for sin. Remember, Lord, Thy promise that he who asks receives, and he that seeks finds, and to him that knocks it shall be opened. I ask, I seek, I beg with all the fervour of my soul. I ask it for every hour of my life; I ask it above all for the hour of my death.

I trust, my God, that thou hast in store for me that merciful Sacrament which is the perfection of the Sacrament of Penance, that Last Anointing which will purify my soul from the remains of sin and heal the wounds and weakness sin has left. Give me by Extreme Unction the strength, the patience, the trust in Thee that I shall need in the hour of my death. Let it comfort me by lessening my fear of death, my sorrow at leaving friends, my dread of the eternity on which I am entering, and the account I have to give. Let it curb the power of the enemy, and enable me to merit greatly by the cheerful acceptance of Thy Will in all my pains of body and mind. I put my trust, dear Lord, in the prayers of Thy Church for me at that hour. That I may profit by them to the full, I will become familiar with them now. So will their sound be welcome at the last, and as She prays Thee by the holy anointing and by Thy most tender mercy to forgive all I have done ill by the misuse of sight, and hearing, of smell, and taste, and touch, my soul will be roused to intelligent response. How much they miss who hear these prayers for the first time when they come to die, who have never troubled to learn what the Church will ask for them in their hour of direst need!

And then will come my Viaticum. There is sweetness, Lord, in all Thy Eucharistic names, but a special tenderness belongs to this. How loving has been Thy solicitude, how abundant Thy provision for those last hours of life on which eternity depends. Sacraments and holy rites fence the deathbed round on every side. And to crown all, Thou comest Thyself and under a new name, the more to arouse our attention, and excite confiding love. Oh, as we lie there on our bed of death, what a pathway of light and grace shall we see stretching back from this Last Communion to the First one long ago!

"Come Thou with Thy servants" (4 Kings 6:3) was our invitation on that bright morning when we prayed

Him to be our Companion along the journey of life. "He answered: I will come. So He went with them" (4 Kings 6:3).

And He has been our faithful Friend and ally all along the road. He has known us under every variety of circumstance. We have welcomed Him as our mood or need suggested, and like a true friend He has fallen in with the exigencies of the hour. As sinners creeping to Him with our burden, as suppliants with our need and our prayer, as hosts mindful of what was His due rather than of our own necessity—thus have we welcomed Him times without number in the Communions of our life. And now the end has come. It is our Last Welcome, summing up all that has gone before. We must meet Him shamefaced and contrite, for now more than ever we want forgiveness and mercy. We must be earnest in supplication, for the moment of our supreme need is at hand. We must exert ourselves to show Him in His last visit such hospitality as our failing powers will allow. Our varied welcomes will commingle in this last reception beneath the veils, which is to herald the face-to-face vision of Himself that will have an eternal thanksgiving.

Lord, let me rehearse today for that hour. Let me win now for my last Communion such grace that, despite weariness and pain, it may be a welcome indeed.

I believe most firmly that in this Sacrament is truly present Jesus Christ, the only-begotten Son of God. Who for us men, and for our salvation, came down from Heaven, and was incarnate by the Holy Ghost of the Virgin Mary, and was made man. In this faith I desire to live and to die. Lord, I believe; increase my faith.

I hope, O my Saviour, in that mercy which brought Thee down from Heaven for me; which has followed me unweariedly throughout my life; which has forgiven me so often; which will continue with me to the end. Yes, my God, in spite of sins, and shabbiness with Thee, of waste of time and grace and opportunities, of neglect of responsibilities, of wrong-doing harmful to the souls whom Thou lovest—in spite of shortcomings of every kind, I hope in Thee, I cling to Thee, I abandon myself to Thee unreservedly for time and for eternity. I know in whom I have believed, and I am certain that He is able to keep that which I have committed to Him. In Thee, O Lord, have I hoped, and I shall never be confounded.

I love Thee, Lord; Thou knowest that I love Thee. Love is shown by a communication of goods. Thou hast given me all Thou hast, giving me Thyself. I offer and restore to Thee all the gifts I have received from Thy hand. I make over to Thee now and for the hour of my death my immortal soul, which Thou hast loved so dearly as to purchase it at the price of Thy blood and life. O dearest Lord, I love and thank Thee for this Thy infinite love; for all Thou hast done for us in Thy suffering life and cruel death; for Thy Church, Thy Sacraments, Thy promises, and above all, for the unspeakable Gift of Thy Real Presence. I love Thee, not only for what Thou hast given and promised, but for what Thou art. I desire to love Thee as Thou deservest to be loved. Increase Thy love in my heart every hour of my life, that I may love Thee in eternity with the whole strength of my whole being, according to Thy desire and mine.

Lord, I am not worthy to receive Thee under my roof. Give me now and for the hour of my death a deep sense of my unworthiness. But let it be true humility with no tincture of discouragement. The less I find in myself on which to rely, the more absolutely will I cast myself on Thy mercy and Thy love.

I desire to receive Thee today, dear Lord, and to give Thee the most loving of welcomes. Give me for my last Communion such faith and fervent desire, that it may rouse my soul from the apathy which numbs the powers and affections at the approach of death. Now and for the hour of my death I invite Thee to my poor heart, uniting my desires to the longing of Thy loving Heart, which desires with desire to give itself to me.

Come, Lord Jesus!

Show me Thy face, and let Thy voice sound in mine ears.

As the hart panteth for the waterbrooks, so panteth my soul for Thee, O God.

For what have I in Heaven, and besides Thee what do I desire upon earth?

Come, Lord, and do not delay.

"Behold, I come quickly."

Even so, come, Lord Jesus!

After Communion

"My God and my Saviour" (Ps. 61:3).

"What have I in Heaven, and besides Thee what do I desire upon earth? Thou art the God of my heart, and the God that is my portion for ever" (Ps. 72:25).

"Bless the Lord, O my soul, and let all that is within me bless His holy Name" (Ps. 102:1).

"Bless the Lord, O my soul, and never forget all He hath done for thee" (*Ibid.*).

"It is good for me to adhere to my God" (Ps. 72:28).

"My God is my Helper, in Him will I put my trust" (Ps. 17:3).

"And now, O Lord, do with me according to Thy will" (Tobias 3:6).

"Protect me under the shadow of Thy wings" (Ps.16:8).

"Show forth Thy wonderful mercies, Thou who savest them that trust in Thee" (Ps. 16:7).

"O Lord, my Helper and my Redeemer" (Ps.18:15).

"The day of Thy inspection, Thy visitation cometh"
(Micheas 7:4).

My God, these words terrify me, for I know my iniquity, and my sin is always before me. I know that Thine eyes see my imperfect being; and if Thou shalt mark iniquity, Lord, who shall stand it?

"Be quiet, fear not, and let not thy heart be afraid" (Isa. 7:4). "I will have mercy on thee more than a mother" (Ecclus. 4:11).

Lord, I fear, not my past sins only, but the rage of my enemy, who will "come down upon me having great wrath, knowing that he hath but a short time" (Apoc. 12:12).

"Fear not, neither be troubled....Is there a God besides Me?" (Isa. 44:8). "Fear not because of him of whom you are greatly afraid: fear him not, for I am with you to save you and to deliver you from his hand" (Jer. 42:11).

Lord, I fear the temptations of that time, the assaults and perils that await my hour of weakness.

"Be not afraid at their presence, for I am with thee to deliver thee" (Jer. 1:8). "The Lord thy God will fight for thee" (Deut. 3:22).

Lord, I fear the loneliness of that hour, for I must go down alone into the dark valley of the shadow of death: no friend may follow me; my need and my cry none will know.

"Abide thou with me; fear not" (1 Kings 22:23). "Thou shalt know that the Lord thy God is a strong and faithful God" (Deut. 7:9). "The friend that will abide with thee in the day of thy trouble" (Ecclus. 6:8). "A friend steadfast" (Ecclus. 6:11). "A strong defence" (Ecclus. 6:14).

I know, O Lord, in whom I have believed, and I am certain that He is able to keep that which I have committed to Him. But I fear lest in the last combat my hold on Thee should relax, and I should fall from Thee and perish.

"Underneath are the everlasting arms. Fear thou not, My servant... neither be dismayed ... for I will save thee ... for I am with thee to save thee" (Deut. 33:27).

Lord, the time for mercy ends with this life. It is as Judge Thou wilt meet me when I appear before Thee, and I am afraid.

"Let not your heart be troubled, and let it not fear" (John 14:27). "It is I" (Matt. 14:27). "Whom having not seen you love, in whom . . . you believe, and believing shall rejoice with joy unspeakable" (1 Pet. 1:8). "I have loved thee with an everlasting love" (Jer. 31:3). "I have called thee by thy name, thou art mine" (Isa.45:4). "I am the Lord and I change not" (Malach. 3:6). "Fear not. It is I" (John 6:20). "Jesus Christ, yesterday, today, and the same for ever" (Heb.13:8).

"The Lord is my light and my salvation, whom shall I fear? The Lord is the protector of my life, of whom shall I be afraid?" (Ps. 26:1).

"If armies in camp should stand together against me, my heart shall not fear" (Ps. 26:3).

"Why shall I fear in the evil day?" (Ps. 48:6).

"Behold, God is my Saviour, I will deal confidently, and will not fear" (Isa. 12:2).

"Though I should walk in the midst of the shadow of death I will fear no evil, for Thou art with me" (Ps. 22:4).

"The Lord is my light . . . He will bring me forth into the light" (Mich. 7:9).

"I will look towards the Lord, I will wait for God my Saviour" (*Ibid.*).

Oblation and Petition, p. 10.

Prayer before a Crucifix, p. 12.

THE LAST WELCOME

II

"In an accepted time have I heard thee, and in the day of salvation have I helped thee. Behold now is the acceptable time: behold now is the day of salvation" —2 Cor. vi.

Before Communion

I LOOK up from my place in Purgatory to the altar rails where I knelt in life, to the place where I made my thanksgiving after Communion. I look back to the moments spent there which perhaps seemed long. Oh for one quarter of an hour now of that "acceptable time"! Oh, to have back one of those "days of salvation"! I realise now to some extent the awful sanctity of God, the frightfulness of sin, the justice of the penalty it entails. Above all, I feel the irresistible attraction of that Beauty of which I had a glimpse at Judgment. I am drawn to it with a vehemence that carries with it my whole being, and flings me upon God as the wave upon the shore. And I am driven back incessantly, for I am not yet ready for the embrace of the All-Holy. The results of sin that might so easily have been thrown off on earth, have to be burnt away here, slowly, painfully, unaided by the least effort on my part. I cry out in my agony: "My God, my God, why hast Thou forsaken me? To the work of Thy hand stretch out Thy right hand! "And He answers me: "In an accepted time I heard thee, and in the day of salvation I helped thee. Oh that thou hadst known in that day of thine the things that were for thy peace. But thou hast not laid these things to thy heart, neither hast thou remembered thy last end. Behold the night is come, in which no man can work. Amen, I say to thee, thou canst not go hence till thou hast paid the last farthing."

How shall I then bewail with unavailing sorrow my neglect of the Treasure provided for me in my Communions wherewith to pay my debts! My Creditor was with me, offering me—nay, pressing upon me—His infinite satisfactions to supply all my need: "You that have no money, come, buy without money and without any price" (Isa. 55:1).

He knows the need I shall have of Him as soon as life here is done. He knows that what we call need at present does not deserve the name; that real need begins in the prisons of the next life, where the soul pines for God with a hunger and thirst of which no craving here can give us the faintest conception. There will be a hunger, too, in His Sacred Heart. They were made for each other, His Heart and mine. "I will draw them with the cords of Adam, with the bands of love" (Osee 11:4). And once the counter-attraction of earth falls away, I shall respond to His drawing with the whole force of my being. Why must I keep Him waiting? Why not use now the riches He places at my disposal? Why not profit by His Presence within my heart to place my cause before Him, to propitiate Him while there is time, while we are together in the way? (Matt. 5).

And why not use my nearness to Him in this life to secure from Him an ever-increasing nearness in eternity and for eternity! How many further degrees of grace are the fruit of one Communion! And to every such degree of grace corresponds a degree of glory, enabling me to know Him better, love Him more, enjoy Him more fully—and that for ever!

"Behold now is the acceptable time, behold now is the day of salvation." Lord Jesus, grant me grace to know in this my day the things that are for my peace!

AFTER COMMUNION

"Holy, Holy, Holy, Lord God of hosts!"

"Thou art Christ, the Son of the living God."

"Thou art worthy, O Lord our God, to receive glory, and honour, and power" (Apoc. 4:11).

And therefore with Angels and Archangels, with Thrones and Dominations, and with all the heavenly army, we sing a hymn to Thy glory saying: "Holy, Holy, Holy, Lord God of hosts. Heaven and earth are full of Thy glory. Hosanna in the highest. Blessed is He that cometh in the Name of the Lord. Hosanna in the highest."

> *"Now is the acceptable time, now is the*
> *day of salvation"* (2 Cor. 6:2).

My Communion Days! O Lord, give me wisdom to use them as I ought. Let Thy close companionship then, effect a union that shall subsist when Thy actual Presence is withdrawn, a union growing ever more real, more intimate, more affectionate, resulting in a gradual merging of all my interests and desires in Thine. Let the love of self give place to the love of Thee, self-seeking to a loyal devotion to Thy Will. Let me search for Thy Will when it is hidden; be quick to see it when it manifests itself; embrace it and adhere to it, even when it brings me pain; rest in it calm and trustful as the bird in its nest. Only thus, Lord, can there be real union between us. And what above all imports is that our relations should be real. There must be no fiction, no shamming, everything must be real between myself and Thee. Life, the soul, eternity, are realities confronting me at every turn. I must face them, and I cannot, I dare not face them alone. As I go on my way my hand must be locked in Thine; my eyes must be fixed on Thee; my feet must follow Thy lead. I must be perfectly true with Thee; my intercourse with Thee must be honest and direct. Thou knowest all that is within me because Thou art my God; because Thou art my Father and my Friend, Thou shalt know it too from myself. There shall be no consciously crooked dealings with Thee; no corners curtained off from Thy sight; no subjects on which it is understood we do not trench. But I will be straightforward with Thee as far as I know myself. If I am mean, selfish, crafty even, I will own to it, at least with Thee. If I am rebellious or cowardly, half-hearted, mistrustful of Thee, Thou shalt hear it all from myself. I will lay bare my heart before Thee that all may be open to Thy sight. I am not afraid that Thine eyes should see my imperfect being (Ps. 138), but only that there should be any willful insincerity, any conscious reserve to check the free flow of my heart, O Father, into Thine.

As I may rehearse for the hour of my death; as I may see myself already amid the penal fires; so I may hear Mass sometimes from within the veil. I may anticipate a little, and from my place in Heaven look down upon the familiar altar whence I so often watch the Sacrifice going up to God. I notice how the act done there rivets the attention of those who live in the full blaze of the unveiled Vision of God; how that white Host attracts the gaze of the whole Church, Triumphant, Suffering, Militant, making all one. The Blessed look down upon It with adoring love; the wistful eyes in Purgatory turn to It in hope; the faithful on earth look up to It as It is raised above their heads, and bow down before the Lamb, "standing as it were slain."

I see the water of life flowing on every side from the earthly throne of the Lamb. It mounts into Heaven and makes glad the City of God. It flows with a strong stream through the arid land of patient pain, and refreshes the sufferers who know at last what the Sacrifice of the altar might have been to them in life, what It might have spared them after death. North and south, east and west, that river traverses the earth, brightening, fertilising on every hand, bringing forth such abundant fruit for God's glory that even now in a measure "the kingdom of this world is become our Lord's and His Christ's" (Apoc. 11:15).

All this I see from my place in Heaven. I see how from the altar where I heard Mass—alas, how distractedly!—the whole Church is vivified and enriched. I see what a more frequent and fervent assistance at that altar in the days of my life would have done for my soul and for those who are dear to me as my soul. . . .

And then I remember with gratitude and great joy that those days are still with me. "The acceptable time" is not past. I may kneel before that altar still. As with the eyes of faith I see above me "the great cloud of witnesses;" as with Angels and Archangels and all the host of Heaven I join in suppliant confession; as I hear the plaintive cry of the captive souls, and my heart thrills with the needs and sorrows of the Church on earth, I understand her termination of all her prayers: "Through our Lord Jesus Christ." I gain a fuller appreciation of the Victim of our altars, the Guest within my breast, and bless God with a new thankfulness for His Unspeakable Gift.

Oblation and Petition, p. 10.

Prayer before a Crucifix, p. 12.

THE LAST WELCOME

III

"Who in his days pleased God"—Ecclus. 44.

BLESSED summary of a life! O Lord, that it might be mine! A few days are granted me, with their flitting light and shade, their alternations of labour and rest, their solemn lessons, their wholesome trials, their tranquil joys—but days only, one and all, passing swiftly with the freight with which I lade them. If I could but remember how fast they speed by, I should not attach myself too much to the pleasures they bring me, not grieve overmuch at their pain. I should think less of the journey than of its term.

Jewish tradition tells of an Eastern prince who sent to King Solomon for a device for a ring that should restrain him in prosperity and uphold him in the day of trial. And Solomon sent him the words: "And this also shall pass away." Behold a greater than Solomon here. Let me ask the Eternal Wisdom who comes to me today to engrave deeply in my heart His word of warning: "Watch!"; His words of comfort: "Be thou faithful unto death, and I will give thee a crown of life" (Apoc. 2:10); "Work your work before the time, and God will give you your reward in His time" (Ecclus. 51:38).

Show me, O Wisdom of God, that the business of this life, the true aim of life is—not success, not honour, not the storing of plenty in view of many years, but to please God in the few days allotted me, by the wise use of all they offer me for His service and for my sanctification.

Let me remember that each day's journey is made once for all. "For behold short years pass away, and I am walking in a path by which I shall not return" (Job 16:23). My concern must be to make each day of march and toil pleasing to God by taking from His hand whatever of joy or sorrow it brings, not attributing to chance, misfortunes that befall me, not stopping at the human instruments by which they come, but passing beyond, to Him who ordereth all things sweetly (Wisd. 8:1). For all my ways are prepared (Judith 9). Nothing upon earth is done without a cause, and sorrow doth not spring out of the ground (Job 5).

My God, when I look upon the holy lives of others, of those who among the heathen are serving thee amid danger and privation of every kind, or, in a sphere of humbler heroism, are bearing nobly the cross of poverty, persecution, failure or sickness, I feel inclined to envy them their generous service, and to look almost with despair on mine.

Yet would I change my lot with theirs? Hardly, I think. Not even for the joy of giving Thee that better, nobler service which they give, could I forego that special knowledge and love of Thee which my past has furnished, and which is my treasure for eternity. Trials, difficulties, weakness, falls, graces, succours, opportunities, victories, joys—Thy patient, persevering love shining through all, guiding all, working out Thy designs through all, could I part with this? Could I part with Thee, *my* God, the God of my life (Ecclus. 23), so sweet, so tender, so true; the God of my experience, dear to me as my own intimate, unshared possession? No, I could not part with Thee, *my* God.

O my God and my Friend! Friend beside whom no other deserves the name; Friend never weary of me, never misinterpreting, never mistrusting, never, like other friends, willing yet powerless; believing all things, hoping all things, enduring all things, I give Thee most humble and most hearty thanks for this gift to me of Thyself.

Thou art a friend that never fallest away. For if we sin we are thine (Wisd. 15), and—as is the wont of the innocent and the injured—Thou art the first to seek reconciliation. O faithful Friend, ever ready with Thy counsel, Thy comfort, Thy warnings, and when needful Thy reproofs, the only friend on whom we can count with certainty, to whom we may unburden ourselves without reserve, with whom there is no waiting for opportune moods and moments, no need of guarded speech, whom there is no fear of scandalising in hours when the heart's bitterness overflows, what shall we render to Thee for all Thou hast rendered unto us in giving us the right to call Thee—Friend!

Thou wert waiting for us when our eyes opened upon this world, and Thy hand will close them gently and lay us to our rest when our work here is done. All through life Thou dost tread the path by our side, and at its points of crisis and of trial we "find Thee there first" (Ecclus. 12:17). O Friend who alone remainest as the road behind us lengthens, and those who began the journey with us have dropped away one by one; Thou who drawest nearer as the gaps widen and the sense of loneliness deepens—stay with us still, stay with us unto the end. The weight of years begins to tell, our steps are faltering—stay with us, stay with us, O Lord! Let the failing of other friendships be the strengthening of Thine. Let the void in so many places make room for Thee, and the instability of all things else drive us to lean with all our weight on Thee.

And when the end is come, when the night falls, stay with us then, O Lord! When the shades of death shut out the sights of earth; when eyes and ears are dulled to the things of sense; when I find myself on the threshold of eternity, and earth has all but rolled away from beneath my feet; when the words of human love no longer reach me, and the voice of Mother Church alone, soothing and protecting, comes between my soul and the perils of that hour—O Friend of my life, show Thyself to me then as the Faithful and True! Prepare me Thyself for the Sacraments in which Thou hast stored help for us in that time of most dire need. Give me such contrition for the sins of my life, that the Last Blessing and Plenary Indulgence may have their full effect, that not all guilt only, but punishment too may be remitted. I shall be equal to little effort, to little prayer, but let my petition now secure me the graces I shall want then. Give me, O Lord, such faith and hope and charity, and such desire to receive Thee, that coming to me in Viaticum Thou mayest strengthen me fully for my last journey, and shield me from the Evil one who will be there with great wrath, knowing that he has but a short time. Lord, all my hope for that last hour is in Thee. I place all my trust in the pity of Thy Sacred Heart, in the intercession of Thy Blessed Mother, of St. Michael, the Prince of all the souls to be received, of my Good Angel, and in the prayers of Thy Church. When I walk through the valley of the shadow of death I will fear no evil, for Thou wilt be with me. Thy Arm will be round me, Thy voice will encourage me— and, dearest Lord, Thy Face will welcome me when the mists of time are cleared away, and in the light of eternity I see Thee as Thou art.

After Communion

"Salvation to our God who sitteth upon the throne, the throne of His glory in Heaven, the throne here on earth of my poor heart."

"O ye Angels of the Lord, bless the Lord; praise and exalt Him above all for ever.

"O ye servants of the Lord, bless the Lord; praise and exalt Him above all for ever."

"Give praise to our God, all ye His servants: and you that fear Him, little and great."

"O give thanks to the Lord because He is good, because His mercy endureth for ever."

*"Fear not the sentence of death . . .
and what shall come upon thee by the good pleasure
of the most High"* (Ecclus. 41:5).

The God of my life I can trust with my death. He who so far has ordered all things sweetly, will not fail me in my greatest need. If death is His sentence, it is also His invitation. As a sentence, justly deserved, I accept it with submission and resignation. As an invitation, I give most hearty thanks for it, and respond to it with gladness. It is the recall from exile, the passage to the Presence Chamber, the gate of my Home. It brings me the unveiled face, the embrace, eternal union with Him whom I love.

Love delights to repay in kind. All through the years of my wayfaring on earth, I have offered Thee hospitality, O Lord. Thou hast stood at the door and knocked, and I have opened. Thou hast asked for shelter, and I have given Thee a home. It is now Thy turn. The time has come for Thee to receive me into Thy House and make me welcome there.

"Lord, where dwellest Thou?"

"Come and see."

"They came and saw where He abode, and they staid with Him that day" (John 1:39).

Answer thus, dear Lord, the longing desire of my heart. Say to me in the hour of my death: "Come and see. For winter is now past, the rain is over and gone, the flowers have appeared in our land. Arise and come (Cant. 2). The long road of exile is nearly traversed; the time of veils and figures, of faith and hope, of struggle, and uncertainty, and fear, draws to a close. Look up and lift up your head, because your redemption is at hand. Look up to your Father's House with its many mansions. I have prepared a place for you, that where I am you may be with Me. Come and see. Eye hath not seen, nor ear heard, neither hath it entered into the heart of man to conceive what God hath prepared for them who love Him: Come and see."

Call me, and bid me come to Thee, O Lord. Call me that I may see where Thou dwellest, and may stay with Thee throughout the day of eternity.

"Fear not the sentence of death . . . and what shall come upon thee by the good pleasure of the most High."

We are told that the best preparation for death is self-abandonment into the hands of God. We have made our peace with Him. We have received Him into our souls who is our peace. What remains for us but to forget ourselves, to leave the care of ourselves entirely to Him. "Fear not what shall come upon thee." Whatever comes will be His good pleasure. Pain of body may come, and anguish of soul. I will lie still in my Father's arms—the Will of God is welcome. Purgatory must come, and it will be grievous and long—the Will of God is welcome. When He shall have fulfilled His Will in me (Job 23) by the cleansing fires, I shall be called to do His Will as it is done in Heaven. I shall hear the voice of my Beloved:

"Arise, My love, and come." "The night is past, the day is at hand" (Rom. 13:12). "Give praise, be glad, and rejoice with all thy heart . . . thou shalt fear evil no more" (Sophon. 3:14). "Put off the garments of thy mourning and affliction, and put on the beauty and honour of that everlasting glory which thou hast from God" (Baruch 5:1). "Arise, make haste, and come."

Oh with what rapture shall I welcome that Will of God, and hold out my arms to Him, and speed away to His embrace. "I have found Him whom my soul loveth" (Cant, 3:3), and now there is nothing to hold me back from Him; "my heart is ready, O God, my heart is ready!" (Ps. 107:2).

Oblation and Petition, pp. 160, 162.

Prayer before a Crucifix, p. 12.

www.ingramcontent.com/pod-product-compliance
Lightning Source LLC
Chambersburg PA
CBHW060241100426
42742CB00011B/1607